Praise for *FROM DEEP SPACE WITH LOVE*
(the original edition of *CHANNELED MESSAGES FROM DEEP SPACE*)

"From Deep Space with Love is really remarkable. I just adored it."

— **SHIRLEY MACLAINE**, actress, author, seeker
Independent Expression Radio, www.ShirleyMacLaine.com

"From Deep Space with Love offers profoundly unique insights that can improve the world, one person at a time."

— **JAMES VAN PRAAGH**, #1 *New York Times* best-selling
author, spiritual teacher, and medium

"If you have ever thought that if you had only known then what you know now, your entire life would have been a far more peaceful and satisfying one, then you must read this beautifully channeled book of wise elders speaking to us from Deep Space who offer just this kind of wisdom. A fascinating, yet immensely practical love letter to we humans, this advanced group of beings collectively called 'Frank' generously shares the wisdom they have acquired, having faced and transcended challenges similar to our own here on Earth. This book is clearly a timely gift to all, and leads to more peace for both ourselves and our planet. I couldn't put it down."

— **SONIA CHOQUETTE**, *New York Times* best-selling
author of *The Answer Is Simple*

"It's not every day you get to communicate with really smart ETs who live 3.6 billion light years away. And even more rare, it seems to me, to find they champion many of the same ideas as me: that being playful is the best expression of ourselves, that stretching boundaries and challenging well-worn systems is a high calling, and that imagination is our most potent superpower. They also picked one of my favorite people to deliver their life-changing message. Thank you, Mike, for being one of those artists, free thinkers, and anarchists (their words) who is open-minded enough to bring us these tectonic teachings."

— **PAM GROUT**, #1 *New York Times* best-selling author of *E-Squared*,
Thank & Grow Rich, and *Art & Soul, Reloaded*

Praise for Tracy Farquhar and Frank

from clients and fans

"The transcendent wisdom of Frank's messages and guidance as voiced through Tracy Farquhar has resonated deeply with me from the first time I heard them speak. . . . Frank approaches every subject with a perspective beyond even what most seasoned spiritual seekers have encountered before. From the meaning of life to the meaning of our current political picture, Frank teaches how we can look at all of our physical experience from the absolute knowing that all is well and that, despite current appearances, there is nothing to fear."

"Frank has such wonderful 'kick in the pants' reminders of how we should be seeing ourselves and our world. I feel so blessed to have you, Tracy Farquhar and Frank, to remind me of these things!"

"I find comfort in the teachings of Frank so often. It makes watching these difficult events so much more peaceful to know that it is all part of the shift and will all work out in the end. Thank you, Tracy Farquhar and Frank."

"Every time I just sit and think about the fact that there are other beings on distant planets willing to share the message of love with us, I feel that love. I'm working on learning to allow its expansion within myself so that I can be a part of spreading love everywhere."

"What Frank means to me is difficult to put into words. The universal perspective presented, the transcendent deep wisdom offered, and the rich thought-provoking guidance given, all support shifts of awareness and being. But for me, foremost, is the vibration of Frank. Behind the words, the grace of the connection and vibration itself moves me deeply."

"Frank has made a vast difference in my life and the lives of everyone they have touched. Their message is one of hope, of vision, of Universal wisdom, of maturity and grounded guidance. I can't say enough about the effect they have had on my own vision and sense of hopefulness, especially with the conditions we are facing in the world today. I am forever grateful to them for coming to us at this pivotal time in our planet's history and to Tracy Farquhar for saying 'Yes' to being their voice and conduit."

CHANNELED MESSAGES

from

DEEP SPACE

ALSO BY MIKE DOOLEY

Books

Love Your Life in 30 Days
Life on Earth*
The Top 10 Things Dead People Want to Tell YOU*
Leveraging the Universe
Manifesting Change
Infinite Possibilities
Choose Them Wisely: Thoughts Become Things!
Notes from the Universe
More Notes from the Universe
Even More Notes from the Universe
An Adventurer's Guide to the Jungles of Time and Space
(formerly titled *Lost in Space*)
Totally Unique Thoughts

DVDs

The Path Less Traveled: Performing Miracles
Manifesting Change: It Couldn't Be Easier
Thoughts Become Things

Video Courses

Playing the Matrix and Getting What You Really Want*
A Trainer's Guide to Infinite Possibilities*

For Children

Your Magical Life
Dreams Come True: All They Need Is You

ALSO BY TRACY FARQUHAR

Frank Talk: A Book of Channeled Wisdom

*Available from Hay House

CHANNELED MESSAGES
from
DEEP SPACE

WISDOM FOR A CHANGING WORLD

MIKE DOOLEY

author of *The Top Ten Things Dead People Want to Tell YOU*

WITH TRACY FARQUHAR

HAY HOUSE, INC.

Carlsbad, California • New York City

London • Sydney • New Delhi

Published in the United States by: Hay House, Inc.: www.hayhouse.com®
Published in Australia by: Hay House Australia Pty. Ltd.: www.hayhouse.com.au
Published in the United Kingdom by: Hay House UK, Ltd.: www.hayhouse.co.uk
Published in India by: Hay House Publishers India: www.hayhouse.co.in

Cover design: Charles McStravick and Bryn Starr Best • *Interior design:* Bryn Starr Best

The Library of Congress has cataloged the earlier edition as follows:

Names: Dooley, Mike, 1961- author.
Title: From deep space with love : a conversation about consciousness, the
    universe, and building a better world / Mike Dooley with Tracy Farquhar.
Description: 1st Edition. | Carlsbad : Hay House, Inc., 2017.
Identifiers: LCCN 2016057554 | ISBN 9781401954024 (hardcover : alk. paper)
Subjects: LCSH: Spirit writings. | Consciousness--Miscellanea. |
    Life--Miscellanea. | Spirituality--Miscellanea.
Classification: LCC BF1290 .D66 2017 | DDC 133.9/3--dc23 LC record available at
https://lccn.loc.gov/2016057554

Tradepaper ISBN: 978-1-4019-5281-5
E-book ISBN: 978-1-4019-5701-8
Audiobook ISBN: 978-1-4019-5700-1

1st edition, May 2017
2nd edition, September 2018

Printed in the United States of America

To the
UNIVERSE,
in all its magnificent forms

CONTENTS

✳

PREFACE

When my mother told me 35 years ago that she'd just read a mind-blowing book explaining reality, supposedly channeled by a lady in trance, whose husband took longhand dictation, I suggested she might be "losing it." I'd always been intrigued by the "far out," but as an accounting major at the time, I was definitely not into the "woo-woo." Mom, however, implored me to read Jane Roberts's *Seth Speaks* and judge the contents not based on where it came from, but for what it said.

I read it. Mom was right. And my life has never been the same.

Channeling, in case you don't know, is the ability to slightly alter one's conscious focus to allow the spiritual energy of another, or that of your higher self, to physically communicate through you. There are many other best-selling works whose authors claim to have channeled them, among them the Abraham books, channeled by Esther Hicks; *Jonathan Livingston Seagull*, channeled by Richard Bach; and countless others. Curiously, many holy books, including the Bible, are accepted by their followers as not written by those whose names appear on the Gospels, but supposedly the word of God or angels, *channeled* through them. Channeling has been around forever.

And now, dear reader, I've got something that just might blow your mind. Its source is absolutely *sensational*, even more shocking than what Mom once shared with me. I'd like to introduce you to "Frank," a collective of eight beings from a planet 3.6 billion light-years away from Earth, in what is considered deep space. To put that in context, many scientists estimate the width of the universe to be 156 billion light-years. Frank is channeled by an acquaintance turned friend, Tracy Farquhar, and "they" (since Frank is plural, not singular) hail not from the spiritual realm, as Seth did or Abraham does, but from the physical realm *upon another planet, right now.* Frank's world, as you'll soon read, is nothing like our world, and they're vastly more advanced than we are in probably every regard, having nearly destroyed themselves millennia ago and lived to tell about it.

Tracy is a professional medium and psychic development teacher who began a journey into discovering her abilities in 2005 when she took classes in psychic development at a local community college. As she worked with her abilities, she became ever more sensitive.

In December 2009, she and her sister were contacted by a collective who identified themselves only as Frank: "We are a group of travelers from the Macelonix galaxy, 3.6 billion light-years away. We have evolved a method of soul transference that allows us to visit other worlds. Our energy is comparable to that of a wave or particle traveling from one point to another. We can transfer it to other dimensions through controlled thought and meditation."

In 2014 Tracy released *Frank Talk: A Book of Channeled Wisdom*, which while fabulously mind-expanding, raised many more questions. I have since had the great privilege of posing those questions to Frank; their answers created the entirety of this book. At first I simply wanted as much information as possible from these distant and, as you're about to read, obviously enlightened guides. Yet with hindsight, I saw that both the questions and their answers were forming a foundation of knowledge and contrast from which any reader could begin imagining how to build a better world here on Earth.

Now, before you shrug this off, I'd like to make a bet that based on your answers to just three little questions, I'll be able to bring you on board. If I lose, you need read no further. If I win, you'll give this book a try.

Deal?

1. DO YOU BELIEVE THAT OUR MINDS ARE MORE
POWERFUL THAN PRESENTLY UNDERSTOOD? THAT WE
LIKELY HAVE LATENT CONSCIOUS ABILITIES THAT NOW
ESCAPE USE, SUCH AS EXTRASENSORY PERCEPTION
(E.G., TELEPATHY, CLAIRVOYANCE, ETC.)?

Sure you do. You've even had your own
supernatural experiences, right? Like knowing who
was calling before you answered the phone. Your
spot-on gut feel. Your treasure trove of insights
offered by the occasional nighttime dream.

2. DO YOU BELIEVE THERE'S PROBABLY LIFE ON OTHER
PLANETS?

Of course you do. To imagine that Earth, among
two to three *trillion* planets—*in the Milky Way galaxy
alone* (as guesstimated by a few scientific geniuses;
the number is not yet knowable)—is the only one
with life, while it alone has many millions of *species*,
is naïve (to be kind). Then consider there are 100
to 300 *billion* more *galaxies!* Meaning the universe
may have 2,500,000,000,000,000,000,000,000
(2.5 trillion x 100 billion) planets! Statistically, if
you could play your local six-number lottery one
time for every planet in the universe, you'd win
178,571,430,000,000,000 times. (The chance of your
winning such is 1 in 14 million.) Which is to say,
hypothetically, if the chance of there being life on
another planet is 1 in every 14,000,000 sampled
(arbitrarily comparing it to winning the lottery,
which you know to be thoroughly daunting), you'd
find life on 178,571,430,000,000,000 other planets.

And then there are all the human eyewitnesses,
photography, videography, and mysterious ancient
ruins that strongly point to our not being alone, and,
yeah . . . of course you do.

3. FINALLY, DO YOU BELIEVE THAT SOME OF THE LIFE "OUT THERE" MIGHT HAVE DEVELOPED THEIR CONSCIOUS ABILITIES TO A FAR GREATER DEGREE THAN WE HAVE?

You have to. I mean, if some can presumably fly spaceships here through technological feats that we can't even comprehend, naturally they'd be more advanced in other areas of creature development. To think that we are the most consciously sophisticated of all life-forms that exist upon 178,571,430,000,000,000 planets calls into *serious question* the intelligence of the life-form drawing such a conclusion—proving the likelihood of the point.

On board?

If so, you're actually ready to go where you've not likely gone before: considering the premise that there are extraterrestrials who've already developed their conscious abilities to such a degree that they've discovered ways to astral project (Google it) to far-flung reaches in space, not only to find us (among others), but to initiate contact. That there are ETs eager to share word of their existence and lessons learned as a species and civilization, solely wanting to be of service. *You'd do the same* if we were to find an attentive, eager-to-learn, primitive tribe in some unexplored jungle on Earth, heretofore oblivious to the modern world. Right?

Sure, some members of the tribe would deny our existence. And some, even if they believed, would probably be riled and not want any such "interference," preferring life as they know it to remain unchanged. Similarly, I'm certain some readers of this book, even some who gave three "Yes!" answers above, will nevertheless be riled by its message and not want any such "interference," preferring life as they now know it to remain unchanged. Fine.

Yet for *your* three yes answers, and the fact that you're still reading, Frank's mere existence is not only probable, but *extremely likely*, to the sextillionth degree. Furthermore, I believe the premises just given, which have been confirmed by Frank, add to this book's authenticity. In other words, while the source of this material is truly sensational, staggering even, Frank's message is *not*. They haven't singled us out to find rare minerals, harvest our DNA, or consume human flesh, as science-fiction films (and perhaps Stephen Hawking) would have us believe. Instead, Frank's intent is to speak from experience on collective cooperation, community, creativity, imagination, love, and self-betterment. Aliens turned big brothers and sisters. Actually, *sophisticated* ETs have probably always been benevolent, just not in our movies. Kindness, I would expect, is a hallmark of *true* sophistication. After all, for any creatures to have patiently developed themselves and their world, emotionally and intellectually, sufficiently to travel space—with grace and good manners no less (whether in their bodies or outside of them)—must have required a discipline and maturity largely unknown on this planet. And to address those who think this book is a ruse to line my and Tracy's pockets with money, don't you think we'd sell a lot more copies if we *were* warning that Frank was after minerals, DNA, and flesh? We'd rather aspire to Frank's sophistication by relaying their insights than try to get rich quick. Not that we'd mind the latter, but our priority is the former.

I deem every word they've offered to be true, for the quality, profundity, and depth of what they share concerning the nature of consciousness. Some of it I already knew to be true; much of it, however, is unknown to the kind of people who would want to perpetuate such as a hoax. Neither crooked extraterrestrials nor crooked humans would *or could* make up some of the things Frank has shared with me on the fly.

Frank claims they are "here" on what we would call a "humanitarian mission": to bring truth and understanding to those seeking deeper insights on reality, given the exciting energy shifts now apparently and evidently happening on our planet. Frank is not here physically, yet they can be summoned at will by Tracy Farquhar. She, like all channels, has developed her conscious abilities to a degree sufficient for "family members" in her energetic alignment to find her. Frank is part of her family, and they are here to help and assist, individually and collectively, as we see in these words of theirs found later in the book:

> *In the unlimited spirit aspect of our beings, we have been able to witness many historical events on your planet, and it is through the understanding of your planet's evolution that we have been motivated to step in and express our perspective on the direction that you are heading and what could be done to improve that trajectory.*

When asked how Tracy could reach Frank at any time—I mean, what if they're sleeping, or in the shower, or mowing the yard when Tracy wants to chat?—Frank explained that like us, they are multidimensional beings, but for their fully developed conscious abilities, they're able to simultaneously lend fragments of their combined consciousness to Tracy, even as they tend to their lives back home. Here are some notes from Tracy on how she channels Frank:

> *The method of channeling Frank can best be described as an intentional relaxation. It is best done during a quiet part of the day, when there can be minimal interruption and noise; many times this will be late at night, just before I go to sleep. I enter a state of relaxation with some deep breathing and, through my intentions, allow a space for Frank to come in. There is a sense that I "step aside" to the left while Frank's energy enters through the right. It is a very gentle and subtle sensation when I am writing, but will be a stronger shift of energy when I channel verbally. In this relaxed state, I will read the question being posed and then close my eyes with my hands on the keyboard of my laptop. The words will come into my head as though they are being dictated to me, and I simply transcribe them as though I were taking dictation. The length of time I can sustain this will depend on how tired I am and my state of mind. Usually, after a few paragraphs, I will stop and do a quick edit for*

*typos, misspellings, and word usage, but I will very rarely tweak
the verbiage.*

*In a live channeling session I once did, an audience member
asked Frank if they could channel in languages other than English, and the answer was quite intriguing. They said that they
communicated through frequency, and not through language,
which means that the energetic frequency they are transmitting
to me as the channel is being automatically interpreted by my
brain into my native language, which happens to be English. If
they were to work with a channel whose native language was
other than English, that is how it would be transcribed. This
also means that the interpretation will be limited to my own
stored vocabulary and word usage; as such, when Frank uses
the male pronoun he, for example, when speaking of Source or
God, this is more of my translation from their frequency than
a literal sense of this energy being referred to as male. Other
words such as people or person, when referring to their own
population, can also be seen as an interpretation of their word
for a collection of beings, and not necessarily as referring to a
collection of human beings.*

I urge you to take these new ideas one at a time—never accepting
anything that doesn't resonate with your own logic and intuition—
and, when ready, to be awed as your mind expands to never before
known dimensions.

Prepare to be subtly astounded,

INTRODUCTION
BY FRANK

We are a group of eight intergalactic beings from a galaxy 3.6 billion light-years from Earth, in a system we call the Macelonix galaxy, photographed by your Hubble telescope and identified as MACS J0416.1-2403. We have devised a method of thought transference by separating an aspect of our spirits from our functioning physical beings and projecting it through the energy of what you refer to as wormholes in space to communicate through this channel, Tracy. It is our intention to assist you with the huge shift in consciousness that is presently occurring in your atmosphere and to help you use this energetic shift to create the changes that will propel your world into a new age.

The existence we experience in our world is unlike anything you experience here, and the physical aspect of our beings is quite different from yours, but our souls are the same, as are the emotional and spiritual lessons we're learning. There is much love among us, as there is among you, and it is at the core of our existence. This love is what drives us to want to help others throughout the universe who struggle with the concepts of love, peace, universal acceptance, and pure consciousness.

This was not always the case, and it took many millennia to reach this state of grace and acceptance of all. We feel that the wisdom we have gained through the near-destruction of our world and the subsequent changes we were inspired to make—which not only saved our world, but created a massive acceleration of spiritual growth, scientific advancement, and compassionate living—can be valuable to those who are willing to listen with an open mind and heart. We feel a great kinship and love for your people, and therefore we feel that our history and wisdom can be imparted in such a way that those who are open to hear it will find the inspiration to shift their own consciousness. We understand that the truth of who we are may be challenging for some, but it is our intention and hope that even those who are resistant to the reality of our beings be nevertheless inspired by our words.

It is with excitement that we engage you through the guidance of Mike Dooley, one of the great spiritual teachers of your age. There are not many in your world today who are able to convey universal truths in such a way that audiences are moved to change the perspective they have on their lives and their world. We have seen that those who follow Mike's work reap great rewards in their own lives, and that others around them also feel the energetic shift that occurs. It is our supreme desire that our combined work will help change the perspective of those who are open to change, and challenge the thinking of those who may not fully realize their own power. We know from the experience of our own people that it is only when we are willing to shift our long-standing perspectives that great change can occur.

On our planet, we found that with our own evolutionary shift came a need for a greater understanding of our power and responsibilities, both individually and collectively, to create the world we were longing for. It was not in the hands of those whom we had seen as authority figures, it was not within the power of the governing bodies, it was not up to the unlimited power of Source, it was within each and every one of us to recognize our own divinity and act upon it. This book will help you to realize this power and harness it, creating an inevitable sense of peace within, power without, and as a collective energy, a shift toward a more balanced and peaceful planet.

There are many guides in your world today who are coming forth to motivate this inspired shift, and it is sacred and divine work they're doing. Regardless of the source, this kind of work is often met with resistance as the masses come to terms with their own ability to create, taking it out of the hands of the unseen and recognizing it as part of their own birthright. There are those who will not understand; allow them. There are those who will ridicule and attempt to shame. Do not give them the energy of your thoughts or any backlash. There are those who will not be able to hear the voice of truth. Allow them, too.

We wish that those who read these pages will ultimately see the limitations of narrow thinking more clearly and stretch their beliefs to include that which challenges the status quo and reveals the true limitless nature of the universe. While some may find it challenging to accept the source of these messages, it is our desire that they go within and experience what we have to say as a form of resonance with their inner truth and their highest knowing. If a truth is felt, does the source really matter? We are connected, we are present, and we come with the highest frequency of love and compassion, which we believe will be felt by those who are open to receive it. Listen, feel the resonance within you, and if it does not feel harmonious with your own soul's frequency, we send you love as you move on. But if it does, we invite you to explore this frequency even more deeply.

Our messages contain the wisdom of experience and a deep faith in the nature of humanity, which we know has the power and potential to achieve all that we have and more. The messages we bring and the questions we will answer all serve that same purpose. If you want to fall in love with yourself, with your life, with your fellow beings, without having to leave the human aspects of your personality behind; if you wish to maintain your selfhood and all its diverse emotions and frailties; if you wish to allow yourself to sometimes fail, sometimes struggle, and sometimes fall without feeling trapped in despair, choose to explore the treasures in your own heart and mind, as this book will help you to do, then you will find the inspiration to embrace all of those imperfections while mining the gold from them and working your way toward a richness of spirit that you've never before experienced.

We are here as ambassadors of light, and we have come for your benefit, but also to fulfill our own destiny, which is to spread the wisdom of the soul that we have discovered through many trials and challenges. We come as humble servants and we come with great love and compassion for all of you, your planet, and all the vast array of living creatures inhabiting it. It is quite a remarkable place, and we hope to inspire you to preserve, enhance, and improve it. Great change is not only possible, it is highly probable, and we wish you to understand your great power to direct that change.

PART 1

LIFE ON BRAHOSHKA

✳

The aim of my questioning in this
section is to reveal the story of Frank's
home planet in earthy terms and
simple language: its near-destruction,
subsequent utopian revival, and the
challenges encountered along the way.
Not that I think we're on the brink of
self-destruction, although I suspect
a thousand years from today,
this optimism may seem
rather naïve indeed.

Are You Similar to Us?

We call our planet Brahoshka (bra-HOSH-ka), although our language is largely unpronounceable to you because of the many physical differences in our methods of speech. It is roughly twice the size of your Earth; however, there are many areas that are uninhabitable, leaving limited areas for our dwellings. This is due to the proximity of our planet to our two stars. The extreme heat and dry atmosphere produced by these stars cause some places of barren and desolate land, which we tend to avoid. Our dwellings are largely underground, as we tend to stay out of the heat and light during those times when our stars are at their closest to the planet, and this assists in their cooling, heating, and protection from the elements. When we are able, we return to the surface to perform ritual and rejoice in the heat and light when it is bearable. Our underground dwellings are quite beautiful, with certain types of artwork and representations of our world that make us feel that the beautiful dwelling we have completed is quite comfortable and love-filled. There are many expressions of talent and beauty in the construction of our dwellings.

The light on our planet is very bright, as the star that provides it is closer than your sun, and so this creates a brightness to our days, which is difficult to explain. This light is experienced as an aspect of the divine, and as such, it can be seen to be like a baptism of sorts when it is very strong. There are many who find it quite beautiful, and our physical reality is sustainable through the resultant heat and light, unlike yours. We worship the divine nature of the light much as some of you worship your God, although we do not have anything like your organized religion. To us, all of life is evidence of the divine nature of the universe and we find great love and comfort in the aspects of our world that are related to the creator.

There are times in our planet's orbit when we are plunged into darkness, but these times are not of the same frequency as yours, and it is during these times that we have great celebrations to represent the bringing of the light. These celebrations honor our ability to bring light into our lives when all around us is at its darkest, and it is a way that we honor the supreme power of creation that lives within us. These periods of darkness have always been seen as sacred times, and we find great joy in the lack of light—and in our ability to light what appears to be empty.

Most of our food is grown in vast covered plots, and some of the growth occurs underground. We also collect water from underground springs and we have discovered many underground bodies of water that ebb and flow just as your vast waterways on Earth. We do not have such vast spaces of water, but there are small ponds and lakes that occasionally appear but then dry up. We are never without enough water, though, as the universe always provides.

The idea of food is not the same as what you experience, as we are entirely plant based and we do not consume any animal products at all. There are certain phyto proteins derived from an algae-like substance that is often dried and powdered and used to create a bread-like food and also used as a thickener and flavoring agent. This is a highly concentrated nutritious agent, which is one of the staples of our diet. There is also a hardy crop of red grain that can be made into a paste and cooked like a cake or bread, and left to ferment for an interesting drink or beverage.

While we are still dependent on the ingestion of nutrition for energy, there is also quite a bit of energy to be derived from the ample light that bathes our planet from our star. There are times when this light is too intense to be directly experienced, but at other times we are encouraged to spend time in the light, as much nutrition and energy is derived from it.

In your Earth years, we live on average 400 years. There are those who have exceeded this by up to 200 years, but most do not exceed 500.

How Old Is Your Civilization?

We estimate through our research that our civilization began approximately 4.2 million star years ago (7.1 million in your years). This predates your human civilization by many thousands of years, and so what seem like advances in our way of life are simply the evolution of culture and technology, and the dissolution of those systems that no longer serve their purpose. Such is the evolution of life; old systems always need to die out to make room for the new. It seems to be the nature of civilized beings, however, to resist change, and so these changes often have many dissenters and sometimes must be gently introduced to those who fear them.

Through our scientific, cultural, and spiritual advancements, we have discovered a way to exist as one with our planet, and to honor it as though it were a living, conscious being, as many of us believe it is. We have learned that treating all conscious beings with respect and care yields much better results than violence and detention, and that loving assistance always goes further than forcing one to conform to societal structures. These lessons were only learned after many different types of systems were shown to be ineffective and failed, leaving researchers with the task of finding those systems that worked in accordance with the laws of nature and not against them. A plant will not grow without the proper care and nutrients. How can a conscious being be expected to flourish in a system that offers little care and support outside the nuclear family? This is where we discovered the greatest results with treating those who were habitual criminals. Through loving kindness, psychological treatment, and a redirection of energy, these offenders were able to be rehabilitated in the vast majority of cases. Those who were not were taken into permanent care in a loving and gentle environment rather than a prison structure.

We look at you as our civilization in its early stages of infancy, and we have so much love for you. Know that all the information we provide is given with the highest intention to help, love, and serve. We have no other motivation to visit and communicate with you than to assist in your planet's evolution.

HOW MANY LIVE ON YOUR PLANET?

There are approximately 8,375,000. This is a slight decrease from previous numbers, as we have advocated controlling the increasing population due to limited living space on our planet. We were once closer to 9,000,000.

WHAT IS YOUR PROFESSION?

We can most closely be seen as aligned with the scientists of your world, although our perspective is quite a bit broader and inclusive of the sciences of spirit, mind, and matter. All eight of this collective have had similar backgrounds. It is through our research and experimentation that we have been successful in the form of spirit transference, which allows us to communicate with you through this channel.

WHAT TECHNOLOGIES HAVE MOST GREATLY IMPACTED YOUR SOCIETY?

One of the greatest discoveries of recent times on our planet is that of a mined type of quartz crystal that has energetic powers unlike anything we have ever before experienced. These energies have been very beneficial to our systems of technology and transport, as they emit their own power, which has been harnessed as an inexhaustible source of energy and is used to power many different types of transport and home systems. These crystals are found in only a few areas of our planet and were stumbled upon completely by accident by explorers who were investigating subterranean forms of life. It was found that some species of cave-dwelling creatures, similar to your crustaceans, were surviving on very little nutritional sustenance other than the energy of these crystals, and so they were studied and examined for their unusual energetic emissions.

With this new energy source, we have been able to eliminate the need for most types of fuel and no longer rely on natural resources that can deplete the conditions of our planet. We have found numerous ways to utilize these crystals and there are still many different aspects of this resource that we are currently researching. It is not unlikely that a similar type of energy source exists on your planet.

Upon these breakthroughs, the onset of telecommunication has created broad-ranging cultural shifts and our technology, while quite different from yours, has created much of the same advances in the fields of education, commerce, and social communication. It was once a fad as it is on your planet, but now it is used much more wisely, at differing times of day for some who wish to entertain themselves with various components of the airwaves.

HOW DO YOU DEAL WITH INTERPERSONAL RELATIONSHIP CHALLENGES?

There is an awareness of self that we have developed through much study and practice, which has transformed the way we handle crisis and disagreements. It is an awareness of the true nature of ourselves that now overrides the need to be right, or the need to be the one with the correct and only truth. This awareness involves the nature of connection between all beings, and this can only be felt and experienced when the mind is at peace and the ego is not in a mode of self-protection. As one works with the higher spiritual aspects of the personality and sense of identity, the ego and intellect are not quite as predominant, thus allowing the soul to provide a clearer view of the situation through intuition and inner knowing. If there is an awareness of the fact that we are all one, the responses to conflict often will not be based on the need to prove that anyone is right or wrong, and will instead provide a different viewpoint of the situation with the intention of helping the other to seriously consider our situation.

This has caused personal relationships to become more integrated and important to our daily lives, but while still maintaining a strong sense of self and the divine nature of our beings, which is essential to the whole. It has created a real balance between mind and body, soul and brain, intellect and emotion. It is here that we are able to function at our peak performance, even while projecting part of our spirit self through a wormhole in space to connect with you. There are great breakthroughs occurring on our planet, even now.

There is also an awareness of the integrated nature of the various components of the soul body and how they work together to form a whole and complete sense of self. Even the love we feel for ourselves when we aren't outwardly successful matching our intentions with our manifestations is extraordinary. True unconditional love occurs when the heart is aligned with the soul, and true self-love is not contingent upon our successes or failures, our appearance, or our ability to attract others. It is an expression of the divine, and it is the basis of all the acts and decisions we make.

There were many adjustments we made to our society as we stressed the importance of unconditional love in all aspects of life, and it was not always easy to get everyone aligned with this new way of thinking. While we did not have the same type of religious zealots that you have, there were many who had their own belief systems that were not conducive to this type of change, and so our recommendations would often fall upon deaf ears. But as tangible results were revealed through this intensive work, many others would join in this group transmutation toward unconditional love as the center of all our actions, and they found that this instilled great happiness and freedom, which they had never experienced before.

There was quite a lot of chaos and a sense of revolution when the government systems fell, but this was quickly abated as new systems developed and were firmly put into place. As others learned that the coup was not self-serving and that the new system truly operated for the good of all, they came to see that this type of heart-centered leadership would be exactly right for our planet and its inhabitants.

In light of the revolutions that occurred in our systems of government, there were many shifts in the seats of power throughout the systems that previously had been the seat of influence. When business structures failed and various types of hierarchy disbanded, the monetary systems were dropped and new systems of commerce emerged that favored barter and many free services such as health care and education. Without a monetary system, there was no more corruption and poverty to be dealt with, and so many of the legal systems and systems of detention and punishment were drastically cut back. Crime is very rare now, and is usually dealt with by finding treatment for its perpetrator, as it is an indication of imbalance and need.

ARE YOU MALE? WHY DO MOST CHANNELED ENERGIES SEEM TO BE MALE?

There are a total of seven distinct genders on our planet, and while you may identify some male characteristics in the method of our channeling, this designation does not correspond with our notion of gender. It is simply an example of how *your* culture tends to designate an assertive and self-confident stance as a male characteristic. The male aspect that appears to be present when we are channeled is simply your own form of gender assignment, which does not actually correspond with ours. The main spokesperson of our collective, the one who is normally the voice of our work, is actually of a gender that bears young, although this is not what we would consider female. We are quite aware of the shifting understanding of gender on your own planet, and it is something that will help to destroy some of the limiting gender stereotypes that tend to hinder the motivation of some of your people who wish to challenge those stereotypes and break free of them but find the acceptance of these attempts to be challenging. As the gender designations become more blurred, you will find that the empowerment of all beings is paramount, rather than a cultural conditioning of gender roles.

Our genders simply do not as neatly correspond to male and female as you might expect. We do not have external sexual organs, and so our identities as such are not as physically apparent as in your world. All of our different gender types are honored and there is no separation or roles assigned to them. Reproduction can be successful in many different ways; our sexuality is expressed quite differently from yours. Still, we are beautiful in our own right; however, our appearance would seem quite shocking to you. Suffice to say that we are very different.

WHAT DO YOU DO FOR FUN?

Our greatest joy comes during our season of ritual and festival, which is during those times when we are able to leave our underground dwellings and venture to the surface of our planet. As mentioned, these times are designated by the proximity of our stars to the planet, and they result in more moderate temperatures and less intense light, which allows us to explore our planet. These times are marked by festivities. At these times, all are encouraged to venture out into the divine light and experience the atmosphere of our planet, which provides some nutrients from its air composition. Also at these times, there is the movement that you would consider dance, a certain aspect of sound that is rhythmic and musical, and a type of singing. It is a celebration of life and we often create quite elaborate festivities at this time. During other times, we derive a great deal of pleasure from playing and storytelling with our young. There are also many group activities that involve debate, communal meals, and a type of game that could be compared to some of your contact sports.

We have quite a lot of live theatrical performances, similar to what you have, but they are open-air performances in which the general public is invited to join in and take part. These performances can run for several days, with various actors and people from the audience stepping forth to continue the action until it is time to end it. There is great hilarity in these shows, and it is a good way to bring our people together and to relax and have fun.

WHO RAISES YOUR CHILDREN?

Children in our society are raised by extended families including the siblings of the parents and the grandparents, who all share equally in the care and guidance of their children. They are taught independence and self-sufficiency early in life so that they can have the courage and strength to survive our somewhat harsh conditions as well as the sometimes difficult personalities they may face as they grow older. There is always a great celebration when a child comes of age and sets out on his own. Children often make long journeys at various times in their lives before they reach maturity so that they can learn to survive on their own and experience different life situations in different locations.

There are many of us who do not live in traditional family roles, and it is not unusual for extended families to share housing and live in a group setting with shared responsibilities for meals and childcare. This type of group living serves us very well, as all share the daily chores so that no one person has to spend all of their time doing the routine necessities and can better pursue other interests. This type of time management ensures that all have equal opportunities for learning and socializing, as well as self-care, and that the necessary chores are still managed. No one is exempt from the care of the home, children, and meal preparation.

PLEASE EXPLAIN HOW YOU VIEW, DEFINE, OR BELIEVE IN GOD— IF AT ALL. DO ALL HAVE THE SAME BELIEFS? IS IT A CONTENTIOUS ISSUE AMONG YOUR POPULATION?

We do not have religions as you understand them, but there was once a sense of contention among those with differing beliefs in our origins and ideas about spirit, energy, and the understanding of what we are. While there has never been a sense of worshipping one divine creator, there have been theories that involved unseen and unknown forces being responsible for the beginnings of our species, and for the universe as a whole. There were stories similar to some of your folklore that revolved around different celestial beings giving birth or creating all that is. And then, of course, there were the scientific theories, which were based solely on what could be seen, verified, and experienced firsthand. Neither of these theoretical bases seemed to be the truth among those who began to understand the energetic nature of reality, and so this is why many of us advocated an expanded scientific view that *included* matters of the spirit, or unseen energy. It was within this investigation that the reality of Source energy began to be more widely accepted as it resonated with an internal sense of truth within us. It was within this expansion of our view beyond that which we were able to physically experience at the time that led to the experimentations with the power of individual energy and its ability to expand beyond the physical limitations of our world.

Our relationship with Source energy is not one of worship, but it is one of great love, respect, and gratitude. And with the understanding that we are not separate from that energy but that we are intrinsically connected to it, we have come to experience the true essence of our nature, which is as a true creative force of the universe.

Do you ever use any mind-altering substances? By the way, is alcohol, for humans, ever beneficial?

While we do not have the same rich and varied diet available to us as you do on your planet, we have been able to develop various mixtures that we find quite pleasurable. There is a process of fermentation that is similar to that which you use in your world to create alcoholic drinks, but it is not quite the same. Our planet provides only sparse vegetation, so some of these plants require some manipulation to create palatable substances. We have a form of water that is a bit different from yours, but still liquid and still necessary for life. There are medicinal substances created from types of underground algae and the manipulated molecules of certain types of what you would refer to as soil. While we do not experience the wide diversity of animal and insect life on our planet as you do, we do have other creatures among us, mostly small, insect-like beings that are ground-dwelling and quite harmless. There are some medicinal substances made from the bodies of some of these creatures, although we are mostly what you would label vegetarians, since as stated, the food substances available to us are quite limited to some types of plants, algae, and another type of growing substance that we can only compare to a type of moss on your planet.

The fermentation of certain substances produces a ritual drink similar to psychotropic substances on your planet, however, without the stigma these substances appear to have for you. These are used in various rituals and for the exploration of consciousness when one is experiencing a troubled state of mind. It is done with the highest intent of healing and finding a peaceful state of mind.

Your fermented alcoholic drinks are quite different from this but we do understand the pleasurable aspects derived from them. Any substance ingested with *skewed intentions* can be harmful. We do not advocate excess in any mind-altering substance, as it separates the consciousness from the truth of the spirit and can cause a depressed state of mind because of that separation. It is this state of separation that causes addiction. However, we do not feel that these substances are detrimental to those who ingest them with a clear intention.

How does time differ for you? Do you experience it linearly, with a single past, present, and future?

Our experience of time is cyclical. The patterns of time correspond with certain aspects of the cosmos, as they do with your own solar system. The difference is that we are able to travel through the various aspects of time and so we no longer feel compelled to designate certain times for certain activities. While time is fixed in our physical experience, the ability we have developed to travel through time and space with the spirit aspect of our being has caused us to work with it in a different way. Time is not a simple, fixed construct, and it is experienced quite differently throughout the universe and throughout your own past and future. The manipulation of time has greatly empowered us to create other changes in scientific experimentation and breakthroughs in health and wellness. It was once as difficult for us to grasp your own concept of time as it likely is for you to understand ours, and so it is clear that the experience of time and its relativity to matter and energy is a malleable one.

DID YOU DEVELOP YOUR HANDLE ON TIME, OR IS IT JUST A
FUNCTION OF YOUR EXISTENCE? DO WE REALLY HAVE A CHOICE
IN HOW WE EXPERIENCE TIME? IF SO, CAN YOU SPECIFY WHAT
MIGHT BE THE ADVANTAGES TO CHANGING OUR VIEW AND EX-
PERIENCE OF TIME?

Because we experience time as a series of cycles, we base our measurements of time on the cyclical nature of life, which flows within a natural rhythm of continual change rather than beginnings and endings. This does not mean that we do not experience the same sort of linear time construct as you, but we do not delineate time in minutes, hours, days, weeks, months, and years as you do. Rather, we observe the cycles of the life of a fellow being as unique to that particular being, while also following certain cycles and rhythms based not only on their age but on the stages of their life, which take them through early childhood, young adulthood, maturity, etc. These cycles do not have a specific beginning or ending; rather, they flow naturally from one to the next, and so we do not measure a person's life by the number of solar years but rather by the current cycle he is experiencing.

The cycles of planetary movement and the appearance and rotation around our suns dictate much of our activity, as we must follow these rhythms in order to proceed safely about our planet. And so it is not the passage of one so-called day into the next that we are too concerned with, but rather the solar cycles, which are cyclical. When our solar cycle is one in which there is sufficient distance of the suns from our planet, we are able to safely travel about, but when the cycle brings the suns close we must remain in our dwellings, as it is unhealthy for us to be exposed to the intensity of that energy.

In order to calculate these cycles, we do not use the same types of mathematical counting of days and weeks; rather, we measure the length of the cycles, which are fairly consistent but not congruent with the sort of day-by-day structure of your Earth.

In this type of time construct, we're afforded a greater awareness of the cycles of nature. We have an improved context through which we can observe the natural rhythm of death and rebirth; the harshness of the environment and gentler seasons; childhood and maturity; and all such cycles that consistently flow from one to the next are celebrated in various ways. Even death is seen as a cause for celebration, as it represents a continuation of the cycles of life, afterlife, rebirth, and life once again.

In many ways, this type of time construct has similarities to yours; however, it is much less rigid and based more on natural rhythms, which ebb and flow and are not quite so predictable as your linear time structure would suggest. This is why your time must be adjusted periodically to take into account the slightly inconsistent movement of your orbit and the magnetic fluctuations that are not always so precise.

Your experience of time, therefore, is very much a choice, and it is within the old beliefs of the cycles of nature and the cosmos that lead to the current structure of minutes leading to hours, days, and years. This is very much a man-made system that strives to create order out of systems that are not always quite so clearly delineated but that create the illusion of a consistency that is easier for your brains to understand and adapt to. Your numerical system with its 10-based structure is also a human construct that originated with the physical structure of the human body. If your physical structure were different, your numerical system would also be quite altered, and so you would experience a different way of counting and mathematical, geometric, and spatially measured reality.

Your system of counting, measurement, and grouping has a huge influence on your time structure and the delineation of time into neat little parcels that are easy to understand and measure. However, it is not always the most accurate and dependable way to structure your lives, as it places constraints and limitations on the being as it passes through stages of age, maturity, and eventual demise.

There is a clear expectation connected with the passage of time, aging, and even the seasons. It is through these expectations that a great deal of stability and comfort is derived when all appears to be proceeding in line with these expectations, but as has been demonstrated on your planet, these expectations are often not met with the patterns of weather, climate, and solar influences on your seasons, in addition to the influences of the individual psyche on the aging process. And so it is within the constraints of time and expectation that you are often finding yourself in the state of frustration and disappointment. We find that a more open and flexible sense of the rhythm of life creates less expectation and therefore less of a sense of frustration when expectations are not met and a sense of instability and fear when the expected rhythms do not go as planned.

While we understand the difficulty and immense global resistance to any changes in your planet's time constructs, we would encourage that you watch the cycles of your natural world as an indicator of the passage of time and the changing cycles of life that flow into each other as an indicator of the progress of life rather than setting expectations of progress based on numerical age, months in the year, or even millennia. Observe your physical reaction to the natural cycles of light and dark, warm and cold, growth and death, without the constraints of a seasonal calendar, which creates somewhat false expectations. Feel how your body responds to different climates when you travel, and how the changing light patterns disrupt sleep and create a sense of disassociation, which can be confusing when one travels great distances. Listen to your body's own rhythms and patterns and observe how they flow both in an individual way and within the structure of a group or community. Here you will find a more natural essence of time in the physical world, and a greater sense of the rightness of all these rhythms.

HOW HAVE YOU MOST SIGNIFICANTLY CHANGED DUE TO YOUR CIVILIZATION'S EVOLUTION?

As a species, we have learned humility, the importance of compassion, the aspect of oneness, and the abolition of greed and a self-serving attitude throughout our transformation. It is through these shifts that we have found true empowerment and stability, which were aspects of our existence largely absent in the millennia preceding this time. Understand that we have evolved emotionally from beings who were largely centered on survival and existence in the harsh conditions of our planet, and it is through that very act of survival that we discovered that the collective was stronger than the individual. However, through the course of our development, we tended to drift from that aspect of oneness to a more hierarchical form of governing and power, which led to the corruption and greed that nearly destroyed us. It was only through the reemergence of that state of the collective consciousness that we were able to find a new way of existence. Individually, we have each discovered within us great power, which has enabled enormous freedom and joy. It is the power of the spirit, or the essence of who we truly are, which has resulted in a transformation of our understanding of all life. While each of us has come from a sense of individuality and unique personality and experience, we each find more power than we ever dreamed possible through the cooperative aspect of the collective. This is one of the things we would like to help you to understand.

How HAVE THESe LESSONS SHOWN UP OUTWARDLY, PHYSICALly, IN YOUR WoRLD?

In the days before we transcended the struggles inherent in the material world, our system suffered many of the same complications that plague your planet. War, disease, crime, and institutional corruption ran rampant, and the future of our system appeared extremely bleak for quite a long while. In the meantime, there were many advances made in the scientific study of the correlation between the mind and the soul, and between the intellect and the consciousness which, it was discovered, is quite separate from thought. It was proven that consciousness, the spirit, the soul, were quite unique energetic components of life, and that these elements were able to be separated from the physical body and the mind in such a way that they could travel through space and time without affecting the existence of the physical life left behind. And so, too, is there another realm of your consciousness that is living a quite different type of life in another dimensional space. This life feels and seems just as real as your waking life does, and in fact, it is just as real, and that is the way you experience it. But you should also have noticed that in your nighttime dream state, your dream experiences also feel just as real and tangible as your waking experiences. So the question could be, which of my life experiences are real and which are not? Our contention is that they are all real, as they all affect your psyche and create the best atmosphere for learning, growth, and ascension.

The lives that we continue to experience share some characteristics with the lives you experience here on Earth, although many of the day-to-day stresses and worries no longer plague us. We have eliminated the need for currency exchange as a means of survival, and so there are no longer issues of poverty and crime related to it. This has become the single most freeing transformation in our world. In our current system, those who are expressing their talents and skills in various ways are encouraged to share these abilities with those who need their services for the greater good. There is *always* an eventual trade-off of services and skills, so the cycle of energetic exchange is never lopsided. What is received will eventually be given, and so the need for a physical manifestation of that energy is merely symbolic and unnecessary. If one performs a large service for another, sometimes gifts will be exchanged in the form of handmade implements and adornments. The elimination of uneven distribution of wealth, the free expression of compassion for all beings, and the unlimited resources of talented individuals who are no longer manipulated by greed have caused exponential growth in the research and development fields, and have created a virtual elimination of high-stress living.

We've also eliminated the need for political hierarchy and oligarchy, and there is a system in place now, which means we no longer need to have a single ruler or leader. In this system, many groups combine to monitor the systems in place with the intention of looking for ways to improve and expand how we offer services and training to the general public. A mandatory, one-size-fits-all, organized educational system does not exist anymore in our world, but because education is seen as a life-sustaining asset, new and varied systems now exist for which attendance is voluntary, yet it is universally available to all and it's seen as quite valuable.

HOW WOULD YOU VALUE THE TIME OF AN AUTHOR, SOMEONE LIKE TRACY OR ME? WHAT IF SOMEONE WRITES A BOOK THAT SELLS A MILLION COPIES? OR, WHAT ABOUT A BOOK THAT TAKES A YEAR TO WRITE BUT IS NOT A COMMERCIAL SUCCESS? HOW IS THE AUTHOR ABLE TO RECOUP THE ENERGY EXPENDED? WILL THE AUTHOR BE DISCOURAGED FROM WRITING IN THE FUTURE?

When it comes to the compensation for creative works such as books, music, works of art, and other items that have a highly subjective sense of value, the issue of compensation is a bit more complicated, but what we have found is that since the value of these items is being determined directly by those who purchase them, and not by any other entity, there is often a greater feeling of fairness in the compensation of time and energy expended.

What we mean is that in your systems as they stand, a book's success (for example) is often determined by the entities that publish and market it, and not necessarily on its merit. Many creative works that are created with great skill are overlooked simply because they are not brought to the public's attention with highly exclusive forms of marketing that may not be easily accessible to the artists producing them. And so we would like to stress that some of the greatest minds and talents can be found in the least examined walks of life, undiscovered by the general public. This does not in any way mean that their work is less valuable; it simply means that those in power have not placed that value upon it.

In our culture, written works are not generally mass-produced as they are in yours; instead, we have institutions much like your lending libraries where written works may be circulated among the public, with additional copies produced based on the work's popularity. Artwork may be acquired by members of the public, but there are also institutions similar to your museums and galleries where certain works may be displayed and viewed. Compensation for these works is not entirely based on the number of people who purchase or acquire the works; rather, there is a system whereby artists of all types are supported in their endeavors with housing, food, and other requirements for living in a sort of colony where they are provided with the materials they need to create within their craft and live a comfortable life. When the works of a particular artist become in high demand, these living arrangements are extended for as long as the artist chooses to produce. If the works do not prove to be popular or in demand among the general public, the artist will be encouraged to pursue some other form of employment while still producing their creative works for the sheer joy of it.

While we acknowledge that not all forms of artistic expression will be performed with the degree of skill and care needed to appeal to the discernment of the public, we will always support the production of creative works simply for the spiritual expansion of the artist and the joy that the creative act brings to their energy. We will provide support for those whose works exhibit the degree of skill and mastery needed to enhance the lives of those who enjoy it, and we will assist those whose works are not as popular to find other forms of employment while still producing that which brings them joy.

WHAT ARE THE TOP five CHALLENGES FACED BY YOUR SOCIETY?

1. **Elder Care** – Our lives extend for the equivalent of 400 of your years or more, and while we generally have good health, there are the issues surrounding an aging population that are similar to those you experience in your society. There is a large population of elderly among us now who need care and attention, and there simply aren't enough

institutions in place to care for them; therefore, many families have taken in their elder relatives and friends to ensure that they are receiving the care they need. Some of these elders not only have challenges with their health and cognizance, they are from an older generation who resisted the changes we instigated, and so some of them are quite bitter and resentful, even though they can see the benefits of the changes that have occurred. This is causing a bit of stress and discontent among the households that have taken them in. We are currently working on the construction of facilities for this population, but it is not easy, as the inhabitable space on our planet is limited and the space needed for this type of construction is difficult to find.

2. **Food Scarcity** – Because of the rather harsh conditions on our planet, there are restrictions on the plant material that is able to grow, and the space in which we are able to propagate it is limited. There have been some breakthroughs in botanical research that have produced new growing methods and new types of plants, but there is some controversy over the use of some of these plants, as there are those who believe they are not natural. This is similar to the issue you are facing with genetically modified plants in your world. Research is ongoing, however, and so far, we have been able to maintain a healthy supply of foodstuff, and we continue to perfect the growing process.

3. **Manufacturing Goods** – As we are restricted in our movement around the planet at certain times, this places limitations on how we manufacture and transport goods. While we value handcrafting more

now than was previously the case, there are some items that benefit from rapid manufacture, and so we do have some types of automated systems similar to your factories, but they cannot be quite as large and they will be restrictive in nature. We do not have as wide a diversity of materials available on our planet as you do; this also limits what we have to work with in the manufacture of items needed for everyday living. The benefit to this is that we have had to become extremely resourceful in the ways we use the available materials, but it does sometimes limit what we are able to accomplish in the manufacture of goods.

4. **Law Enforcement** – While we have been experiencing one of the most peaceful eras in our history, there is still a need for "peace officers" to uphold the law and maintain order. There are some issues that arise from this need, which are somewhat similar to the issues you experience on your planet. While we do not have many issues involving violence, we do experience the occasional theft or disturbance that requires the intervention of law enforcement. We are continuing to work toward a culture that is free from violence, but at the present time, we do experience certain expressions of anger or reactions to perceived slights that can lead to emotional outbursts and worse. The issues arise here when the officers become overwhelmed with the sense of power and either abuse that power or withdraw from it.

5. **Damage Done to the Planet** – Before we were able to shift our consciousness into one that honored our planet and the land that we live upon, there were some forms of industry that were doing quite

a bit of harm to the structure of the planet through mining, experimenting on the soil, and blasting through sedimentary rock in search of resources. While multiple efforts are continuing to be made to heal some of this damage, it is clear that some of it is irreversible at this time. There are areas of instability in the land as a result of some of these destructive practices, which again places limitations on the areas of our planet that are habitable and safe. We are confident, however, that we will continue to heal from these catastrophes.

WHAT ARE THE TOP 10 WAYS YOUR SOCIETY DIFFERS FROM OURS?

We are happy to compile a list for you. Understand that the comparison is by no means meant to offer criticism or judgment of the systems currently in place within the structure of your culture; it is merely to offer an alternative perspective. This is what we hope to achieve through these communications: a sense that there are other methods of living that can create more balance, cooperation, and heart-centered living. It is our hope that our examples will motivate you to find your own.

1. **Monetary Exchange** – As we've stated, we do not operate within the structure of a monetary exchange for goods or services. Once we identified that the use of currency had created a huge sense of inequity and materialism in our culture, we made it a priority to devise other systems that created a more balanced method of energetic exchange. We identified the true nature of currency as a symbol of exchange, rather than a method of material gain, so we were able to find other methods of exchange that do not as greatly affect a class structure favoring

those who have the means to accumulate wealth over those who do not. A simplified explanation of our current system is one in which each individual is able to focus on their strengths, talents, and gifts in order to provide goods and services to fulfill the needs of the community. There are some who work in communion with others, and some who are more solitary, just as in your society. For instance, if one is drawn to running a storefront that provides a certain type of goods, there will be a system of checks and balances kept that records the goods taken. Those who take the goods will be beholden to provide their own merchandise or services in exchange. This is not always a direct exchange, however, as these types of institutions are usually managed by a group cooperative and so the exchange can occur among any members of that cooperative. There is a great deal of trust built into this system; we have found that the vast majority of individuals honor it and gladly maintain the balance of exchange without having to earn and spend any type of currency. There are also systems in place to care for those who are unable to work for whatever reason; however, we find that more people are motivated to find some sort of occupational activity, no matter how limited they are, which somehow contributes to the well-being of the society.

2. **Marriage and Relationships** – Our culture does not have the ritual of marriage as part of the family structure. As a community-based society, family structures can be extensive and include those who are not related by birth but are those with whom we choose to share our lives and sometimes our homes. While there are those who choose to have

monogamous relationships, it is not the only cultural standard, and there are some who choose a less structured form of relationship, just as there are in your culture. We do not have the same standards regarding sexual behavior, as it is not viewed in quite the same way in our culture. So many of what you may view as moral standards simply do not exist in our culture, and we operate quite well within this system. Acts of physical affection are not limited to sexuality, and so there is less of a sense of having all needs met by one partner or one spouse, and instead there is less of a formally structured foundation in the area of relationships. This does not mean that we are not respectful and sensitive to the emotional and physical desires of others; it simply means there are fewer expectations on romantic relationships as the major source of stability and happiness. Love is not reserved only for those to whom we are bound in a sense of formal ritual; it is something we express more freely, but not necessarily in a sexual way. While there is a sexual element to relationships and of course to the act of procreation, it is not emphasized quite so much in our culture as the only means of showing affection, and it is not regulated quite so much by our standards of cultural behavior. It exists more as a natural form of self-expression, which, while still being a private act, does not have the underlying sense of sinfulness attached to it and therefore does not have industries, businesses, and exploitation attached to it. We would like you to consider how a shift in this area may create huge changes in your own world's culture.

3. **Health** – Since we do not have a monetary system of exchange, the areas of health and wellness are

not structured as profit-making businesses. As such, our emphasis is more on the wellness aspects of health rather than an industry of pharmaceuticals. Those who have serious issues of health are cared for and supported nutritionally in such a way that the balance is brought back to the body so that it is in the best energetic environment to heal itself. While we will use certain forms of plant-based medicines to help balance the body's systems, alleviate pain, and discourage the growth of foreign invaders to the body, we do not have the wide range of symptom relievers available in your culture, as we feel that it is the symptoms that can help to identify what the body needs to support its healing. In other words, we do what we can to make the individual comfortable and we provide care that involves meeting nutritional needs that will strengthen the physical systems so that they can heal. As we have eliminated a lot of the toxins that cause many of the forms of disease we had previously been experiencing, we have had a huge decline in health problems among our civilization, and as the levels of stress in our daily lives has diminished, so have stress-related illnesses. This does not mean that we do not experience illness; it simply means that we no longer have the need to create an industry structured on sickness,[1] and as such, there is a cultural system now that is based on maintaining wellness. We have found that this has created an environment of fewer incurable diseases, less of a need for medical or medicinal intervention, and longer life spans. There has also been a decline

---

[1]   A case in point concerning cystic fibrosis was offered by Frank and is included in Part 2.

of illness among the elderly, and many continue
to live quite robust lives until they are ready to
transition forward. We are pleased to see a gradual
shift in attitude toward health and wellness in your
own culture, although there is still much work to be
done in the areas of integrating forms of energetic
health with physical health, and moving away from a
system of profit-based pharmaceuticals.

4. **Political Structure** – The foundational structure
    of leadership based on hierarchy, status, and wealth
    was one of the main components of our society's
    near-collapse. As these systems of leadership began to
    crumble and decisions became more based on greed
    and gain rather than the common good, the entire
    structure of society collapsed and we were forced to
    create an entirely different structure that would rise
    up against much opposition and fear. We have seen
    similar scenarios played out in the history of your
    world's culture, and we are aware of how the collapse
    of these systems has often resulted in great acts of
    violence and suffering for those who were dwelling
    within those structures. It is quite remarkable that
    your culture has recovered, time and time again,
    from these disasters, and we see this as evidence that
    there is a core foundation of those who see the truth
    and who really do have the common good as the
    foundation of leadership. Power is quite a challenging
    aspect of leadership, as it activates the ego in such a
    way that it begins to use fear as its motivating force.
    As such, we have developed a more even distribution
    of power that is not focused on one person's ability to
    make decisions that affect many, but rather is a true
    commonwealth led by those who have demonstrated
    their abilities to create change that is in the highest
    good of all, and not just for self-serving needs. This

type of communal structure is not party-based, nor is it based on votes or family lineage, but rather on a demonstrated ability to have foresight, intelligence, intuition, and compassion as the basis for their decision making in all areas of their lives. Individuals can be nominated or apply for these positions, and a code of standards is followed to choose those who are best suited to these positions. These officials are not seen as status symbols or high-ranking individuals; rather, they are seen as citizens with extraordinary intuitive gifts to understand what is needed and creative gifts to usher in needed change. Without a monetary system, which can be the foundation for greed, these officials are more likely to stay true to their intentions and loyal to the individuals they serve, and as there is an equal distribution of this power, it is unlikely that one will be guided by the self-serving ego.

5. **Education** – Our structure of early education has become much more relaxed and less rigid than it once was, which allows for more freedom of expression, individual growth, and blossoming of spirit. We discovered that when forced into a structure that treated all as one standard, without leaving allowances for different styles of learning and different personalities, there was a resistance to learning and a rebellion against that forced standard of behavior. As we began to allow more free time for movement, creative expression, and unstructured play and discussion, the students responded in a much more positive way, as their individual characteristics were honored and their need for physical movement and an open forum for free expression were respected. We found that

with less pressure and structure, students were more prone to a better learning experience and their eagerness to experiment with new ways of thinking through a hands-on approach was remarkable. The secondary educational system was completely destructured into more of a trade school type of institution, which allows a broad scope of experience and few requirements. Those who wish to learn a particular trade can concentrate solely on the training that is geared to those skills, and those who wish to experience a broader scope of learning can pursue this with impunity. Learning is encouraged throughout the life of an individual, and so there are students of all ages to be found in these schools, many of whom are pursuing education simply for the enrichment of their lives and for the experience of expanding their minds. There are few to no expectations for secondary education; students are encouraged to seek out that which emphasizes their own unique skills and talents, and to pursue different paths throughout their lives for a rich and varied experience. And again, without the binding goal of profit and income, these schools can be more focused on their main intention and do not need to sell their services, and students do not have the pressure of debt to interfere with the enjoyment of the experience.

6. **Spirituality and Religion** – While we never had the same type of religious structure that is prevalent in your society, we did at one time have some structures of belief that were more readily accepted than others, leaving those who practiced outside of those structures to feel left out or judged. There were those who practiced a more spiritually based type

of belief system and those who adhered to a more
standard practice of ritual and belief, with little scope
between them. The numbers who practiced the more
structured belief system began to dwindle as our
societal structures gave more respect to the individual
and placed a greater emphasis on cooperation.
Within these new structures came a need for a type
of spirituality that honored the individual, rather
than punished it, and created a more supportive
framework of the community, without judgment
or a sense of sinfulness. Thus, we now have a more
spiritually based society with many levels of belief,
all based on the idea of rejoicing in a sense of
gratitude, honoring the Divine Spirit, acknowledging
the spirit that lies within, and celebrating the
transition of this spirit upon the death of the body.
Not everyone practices ritual or worship, and there
is no sense of a right or wrong way to practice
spirituality within this structure. Similar to the way
the educational system was changed, the freedom
of expression in the spiritual community has caused
a peaceful coexistence which no longer judges or
forces those who practice into certain structures of
ritual. Gatherings are held for those who wish to
express their love for the creator in that way, and
solitary practice is found among those who feel more
comfortable with that. Some do not participate in
any structure of belief, and some find a daily practice
of ritual to be soothing and beneficial to their state
of mind. All are welcome to express this sense of
themselves in any way that suits them, and there is
no labeled delineation among these forms of spiritual
expression.

7. **Food and Nutrition** – As we have previously stated,
    our nutritional sources are not as varied as yours;
    however, we find that with some creativity, we are
    able to experience a diverse and interesting diet that
    has the density of nutrition needed to survive the
    harsh conditions of our environment. There was
    never a time in our world when we had the systems
    of manufacture that we currently see in your world,
    although there are processing areas for different foods
    that require it. We have always had to be conscious
    of maintaining a nutritional diet, and so we have
    not experienced some of the issues your world has
    encountered with a prevalence of less nutritional
    and habit-forming foods, and there are no standards
    of beauty that emphasize a certain body structure
    or weight. However, in the changing structures of
    our society, we found new ways of processing the
    limited resources we have, which preserved the spaces
    in which these things are grown and cultivated,
    and increased production through more careful
    harvesting and more strategic farming. We have
    also developed some new species of food material
    that is more nutritionally dense and covers a wider
    range of needs molecularly. This has not required
    genetic engineering, however; instead, it involved
    a propagation of a current species of plant that was
    once considered inedible in such a way that allowed it
    to be ground into an edible form with the application
    of heat to dry and crush it. We have also discovered
    some other flowering plants that yield a variety of
    edible material that can be compared to your fruits.
    These additions to our diet have added a nutritional
    source that is helping to increase the health of our
    population and the awareness of the need for a rich

and varied diet has grown with education and the increased availability of products. Again, without the profit margin placed on the manufacture of food, more emphasis can be placed on its nutritional value rather than its habit-forming appeal.

8. **Science and Technology** – Once again, this is an area that has benefited from a relaxing of standards and a broadening of scope, which has stretched to include the research of previously uncharted territory in the areas of scientific exploration. Once scientists were able to cross the line from pure scientific inquiry to include the research of energetic spirit, the science of thought, and the power of the energetic realms, everything we had previously believed to be true within the rigid structure of scientific inquiry changed. We find many similarities in this structure with your own, and so this is an area where we see a great deal of scope for expansion and change. Once the areas of research began to expand beyond that which was once deemed possible, new systems were found that could be harnessed for things that were previously only dreamed of. New technologies that were once thought impossible were borne from the study of energy and from the exploration of the energetic fields of deep space. These methods of exploration were only possible through the energetic expansion of the individual's spirit being, and so just as we are able to communicate with you through this energetic transference, there were amazing things discovered about the universe through the same type of exploration. Removing the physical aspects of space exploration has eliminated the need for physical transport and the time and space constraints inherent with that. It has also opened up fields of

molecular and atomic exploration within the physical structures of our planet and our own bodies, which was never even thought of previously. The power of the mind and spirit is still being discovered in all its varied nuances and complexities and it is a field of research that is ever expanding in its scope.

9. **Energy and Fuel** – There was once a form of energy that was mined on our planet in a similar manner that your fossil fuels are currently extracted from the earth. Our energy needs are quite different from yours, but there still exists a need for fuel and we were finding that the extraction of these fuels was damaging our environment, which was already limited in its habitable space. Once it was determined that a new system of fuel was required, new research was done to experiment with different types of material from our planet's physical structure that had not ever been experimented with as a possible form of energetic fuel. It was in this research that different types of crystalline structures, originally found while investigating subterranean forms of life as previously shared, were experimented with and we were able to discover one type of crystal that emitted its own form of energy that could be harnessed in an unlimited way. This discovery changed the way we utilize energy forever, and there is no longer the need for destructive types of mining and the scarring of the land in order to extract vast quantities of fuel. A small number of these crystals is all that is needed for huge amounts of energy, and these crystals do not require replacement for long periods of time, so our land is preserved and the energy is produced in a clean and predictable manner. The research that discovered this type of fuel would not have occurred

had there not been a crisis in the environment
and a dire need for change. We would suggest that
your researchers expand their scope beyond the
profit margin to seek out a similar type of energy
alternative.

10. **Entertainment and Leisure** – Our current
structures of work, education, and family allow for
more free time and there is more emphasis placed on
the need for leisure and relaxation. This has created
new industries that are geared toward pleasurable,
interesting, and relaxing pursuits, which help to
quiet the mind while allowing for a stimulation of
learning and a wide range of self-expression. Artistic
and creative pursuits are highly encouraged, so there
are many programs for those who wish to spend
time creating art and music. Large groups will gather
for cooperative projects involving dance, art, and
music. Many forms of writing as an art form are
experimented with and again, groups have emerged
who have created unique forms of literature and
expressive verse. There are groups that work with
the art of dreaming, and those who use telepathic
thought as a means of creation. Science has created
methods to make thought forms visible, creating a
sort of performance art that is quite incredible, and
new methods of expressive movement are always
being performed in public forums. There is a culture
of artistic expression that is richer than it has ever
been in our world, and this has not only created
more beauty and emotional healing in our culture, it
has created a flow of energy that has benefited all in
myriad ways.

GIVEN YOUR CIVILIZATION'S RISE AND SUCCESS, CAN YOU SHARE WHAT THEY WOULD VIEW AS THE 10 MOST IMPORTANT VALUES A SOCIETY OR AN INDIVIDUAL CAN HAVE AND HONOR TO BE HAPPY AND SUCCESSFUL?

We are quite delighted with this question and all that it implies. It is quite true that we discovered, through the deliberate and intentional shift of the trajectory of our civilization, that there were certain values and aspects of being that were vital to that shift, and that many of them had been quite lacking in the periods of our society's degradation:

1. **Self-Expression** – This is the greatest strength of the individual and of a thriving society as a whole. It is the aspect of the individual that is most suppressed in societies that seek to create a sense of blind obedience and mindless consumerism. The institutional influences on the will of the individual will often seek to devalue the inherent gifts, talents, and passions of the individual in favor of a lifestyle that forces the individual into a more traditional role of wage earner, consumer, and rule follower. Self-expression can be seen to be dangerous to that type of institutionalized structure; creativity will be undervalued, and those who operate outside of a created structure of limitations will be viewed as delusional or dysfunctional. Structures will be put into place that create deliberate divisions in that structure; those who fit in will find their sense of identity with the crowd, while those who do not will be outcast and left to find their own sense of identity. You can see numerous examples of this structure in your own culture, and yet you can also see how the shift is beginning to create a sense of wonder and reverence for the misfit, rather than an automatic

derision. The free-thinking creatives who truly live outside the perceived and invented structures of categorized behavior, standards of beauty and worth, financial status, and intellectual standards are the forerunners of the new age in which the entire structure of what is valued, deemed worthy, and admired shifts toward a more genuine and heart-centered form of self-expression.

2. **Self-Worth** – Self-expression is not possible without a sense of the intrinsic value one feels for one's sense of self, one's dreams and desires, one's abilities and gifts. Once again, the society that is structured to devalue the individual with the intention to have better control over it will seek to create a perpetual state of lack within that individual. The idealized sense of perfection that is held up as the ultimate goal of life is deliberately unattainable, and will cause those who adapt this into their lives as truth to suffer a never-ending sense of lack, which causes them to continually seek to fill that void with consumerism and unhealthy behavior. As your society begins its shift toward a more compassionate, heart-centered, and resonant way of being, the individual will begin to understand the intrinsic value of their own being to the whole, and will be more prone to follow the desires of the heart toward self-expression. And while not all who begin to move toward a stronger sense of self-worth will comprehend it, they are, in this journey, becoming more aware of their direct connection to Source and conscious understanding that their growing sense of self-worth and self-expression is the ultimate celebration of the divine within.

3. **Service** – In a culture that seeks to dominate rather than encourage the individual, the values of self-expression and self-worth will be deemed as acts of selfishness, self-centeredness, and sinful conceit. In fact, it is a natural aspect of these values to have the desire to use them in service to others, since this is a value that resonates most harmoniously with the frequency of the spirit and the attunement of the heart. Those individuals who are most removed from their sense of self-worth and self-expression will live in a perpetual unconscious state, and so will have no connection to their heart's desire to be of service. They will be the ones who are continually seeking outside of themselves to fill the perceived voids in their beings; it is through that distraction that they will navigate their life path blindly, with little regard for how their behavior and energy affect others and the world around them. It is those who are truly in touch with the divine expression of their being who will most deeply feel the urge to be of service and use their intrinsic gifts to enlighten, uplift, comfort, and express compassion to all they come across. They will be the ones who create beauty, useful technology, new systems, and better institutions. They will instinctively feel what is needed and will find ways to fulfill those needs with their gifts. Being of service creates a natural state of joy that is not possible in any other way; those who rarely experience this state of joy are missing that experience only because they are not experiencing the true connection of their divine will with Source energy. All beings will be given the opportunity to be of service at various points in their lives; not all will heed this call, but those who do will find the highest form of fulfillment, passion, and lust for the divine expression of life.

4. **Compassion** – This is a value that is often misunderstood to mean suffering for others in their pain. The compassion that we are referring to here is simply a heart-centered connection to others through the realization that all beings are intrinsically connected by and to Source energy, and as such, there is an aspect of ourselves in all others. While this type of compassion can sometimes allow us to feel the pain of others, it is not in the feeling of that pain that healing can occur; rather, it is in the feeling of that pain that we are motivated to act in a way that eases the pain of the other in whatever way is available to us. Truly compassionate beings do not feel the need to heal, save, or rescue other beings from their situations; rather, they seek to uplift, empower, and motivate those individuals to find their own inner sense of peace and truth. Taking on the ills of the world is not a true expression of compassion, as it does not ease the suffering. In fact, it expands it as we pass it on to others through our energetic expression in the world. True compassion leads to a sense of service, which is intrinsically connected to the sense of value one has for one's own gifts, and the need to express those gifts in the world. If one is expressing a certain talent or gift in the world, and understanding the value of it, one will automatically be drawn into putting those gifts into service to others through acts of compassion. Expressing these values every day, in the smallest acts of kindness and in larger acts of extreme service, creates the same ripple effect of energetic connection between all beings, and starts the cycle of compassionate action that will ultimately be the force that shifts the energy of your culture into a different realm.

5. **Playfulness** – In the daily routine of the institutionalized culture, this is a value that is sorely undervalued and severely lacking. In the seriousness of the workplace, the focus on tragedy and horror in the media, and society's anticipation of impending doom, there is a sense that playfulness creates a trivialization of life and ignores all that is wrong and needing attention. The truth is that in the temporary nature of your physical existence, all that you are focused on as tragic, horrific, or evil are simply *aspects* of a *transitory* existence. More, this focus then blinds you to all else, including the overwhelming predominance of all that's good and beautiful in your existence. You thereby become unable to find joy in your daily existence, creating a culture of routines and hopelessness. When we are playful, we are in the midst of our most highly creative expressions of ourselves; we are opening the channels to higher wisdom and guidance through the energetic flow that is created in the act of play. It causes us to drop barriers, cease trying to control, and simply allow an energetic flow of joyful expression. This is where you will truly find your most authentic nature, and your highest connection to divine wisdom. Children experience this state continuously by design, as they are in an accelerated state of evolution and learning in their early years. As play becomes more discouraged and seen as an expression of immaturity, learning slows and creativity is squelched. As we brought play back into our culture, we found that it strengthened not only the individual connection to self-expression but also the sense of cooperation and a true sense of connection with all beings.

6. **Patience** – As the pace of life accelerates with your
advances in technology, you then experience a false
sense of urgency with regard to all else in life. Which
leads to a growing sense that you are running out
of time, both individually and as a planet, and the
need for instant gratification; the virtue of patience is
slipping by the wayside. The act of waiting can be a
moment of Zen-like peace, or it can be a frustrating,
frantic experience of irritation and aggravation.
The art of slowly moving toward one's goal is no
longer seen as an advantage, as it always appears
that someone else will come up from behind and
overtake you. The act of creation, however, is a
process needing time to coalesce and respond to
the frequencies that are creating it. In the mind
of one whose very nature is based on impatience,
everything appears to be moving in slow motion, and
the main complaint is that everyone should move
just a little bit faster. The expectation that all things
should come to fruition in a quick and predictable
way causes one to be continually anxious about
reaching goals that are perpetually out of reach.
This forward-thinking energy is often admired, as
you believe that these types of people are the real
innovators and that they are the ones who will create
the changes in your world. However, we would like
to point out that the stress placed on the body and
mind by continually looking toward what's next
not only affects the health of the individual, it also
creates huge rifts between the personalities of those
who are forever looking at the future and those who
are just trying to navigate through their current life
situations. Patience does not only mean waiting for
life to happen to you, it means understanding that

the journey forward is where life occurs, and that you will never reach the end of the journey, even when the current leg of that journey ends.

7. **Allowance** – Along with diminishing patience is the need to control; much of your society's ills can be traced to a pathological need to control all events and other people. In this type of personality, there will be tremendous stress felt in the body and mind when it appears that circumstances are out of one's control. While it is true that you are all co-creators of all you see, that does not mean that these creations will appear overnight, or that you must feel a compulsive urge to continually churn out the manifestations of your imagination. To those who have trouble relinquishing control, we suggest this: Imagine yourself on a rowboat alone, and you are paddling against the current. You will soon realize that all the work you're doing paddling has only landed you back where you came from. Understand that a great deal of your creative influence is initiated through your energetic intentions, and that there is the potential for much peace and flow if you begin the process though the energetic field of intentions and leave the rest of the creating up to the universe. If you express a desire or dream, allow yourself to believe that the Creator has heard you and that you will begin to receive some valuable guidance at any time. Building up excitement toward what's to come, rather than picking apart whatever it is that you've created, is the hallmark of the joy of abundance and the full expression of one's soul. Pull up the oars, trust the current, and simply dip the oars in occasionally to steer. Allow ease and flow into your life, and you will find that things will come much more easily to you.

8. **Flexibility** – As with allowance, being flexible
    creates a sense of ease in the process of creating, and
    it removes rigid expectations that can cause so much
    suffering. When one remains flexible with what they
    believe to be right or wrong, good or bad, desirable
    or repulsive, one will find the best way to create a
    compassionate and forgiving environment within
    which to practice kindness and co-creation. Rigid
    views, narrow expectations, and a black-and-white
    stance on right and wrong create enormous stress on
    the mind and body, since the natural laws dictate
    a balance of give and take, straight and winding
    roads, and predictable and so-called strange behavior
    of others. Think of the fluidity of the body in acts
    such as dance, yoga, and gymnastics; if the body
    were to remain rigid and unyielding, the beauty of
    these practices would not be possible. Your life path
    is such that it will afford you a myriad of different
    and sometimes challenging experiences that offer
    the opportunity to grow, learn, and evolve the mind,
    body, and soul. If these lessons are avoided out of a
    rigid sense of judgment based on outward or surface
    experience, frustration and a sense that you should
    be thinking of doing something else will ensue,
    leaving you with little energy to place yourself out
    into the wider world. One can bend while staying
    true to one's intentions; one can flex while not
    allowing cruel or unjustified behavior. You can move
    through those events that challenge you the most
    without trying to force the circumstances themselves.

9. **An Open Mind** – Practicing flexibility and patience
    can lead to the phenomenon known as an open
    mind. Too often, we find that humans tend toward
    believing that their aspects of being should contain

very staunch and rigid views on certain social and world events. There can be a very rigid sense of what is right and wrong, and the ensuing judgment that arises from this viewpoint can close a mind to the flow of energetic information that is available to all. It is the closed minds of researchers, scholars, and medical practitioners that have prevented them from seeing the real truths that are already being felt by many. It is through the rigid stance that only certain aspects of life are "real" and others are either the product of imagination or psychosis that disrupts the connection to the energetic field of the divine and the energetic field of others. As such, the institutions of education, medicine, and business all encourage a closed-minded aspect of reality that is based on the interpretations of the fallible brain and the somewhat arrogant stance of one who judges. Maintaining an open mind, while still practicing discernment, can be the key to your survival.

10. **Imagination** – The process of all creation begins with the imagination, which is a form of consciousness in direct connection with the higher vibrations of spirit and Source. It is within the moments of active imagination that all great things are birthed, and where the very universe came to be. However, the imagination is often downplayed as a place of fantasy and mirth that is not relevant to the "real" life experience. By claiming that some experiences are "just imagination," you are negating one of the purest and deepest connections to Divine Source energy and the energy of the higher self in all of its creative power. When the imagination is stimulated through self-expression,

play, and creative pursuits, that direct channel is opened and all possibilities will come pouring into the consciousness. We would recommend that the term *imagination* no longer be vilified, and that it be encouraged in all walks of life, from childhood education to higher learning, in the workplace and in the home. Storytelling, music, writing, and the arts are wonderful ways to build the powers of the imagination and understand their value.

WHAT ARE THE TOP 10 DREAMS OR GOALS OF YOUR PLANET'S INHABITANTS?

Although we have overcome many of the challenges that were leading us on a path of destruction, the individual dreams and goals of our inhabitants are not that much different from yours. In fact, our experience has shown that all beings in the physical state with higher consciousness desire many of the same things.

1. **Peace of Mind** – Even though the everyday stresses of living have been greatly reduced by the changes we have made in our society, there are still other worries and concerns that can disturb the peaceful state of mind that many strive for. We continue to be concerned about the state of our planet and its future, and we are concerned for our children and what their lives will be like as they mature. There are still those who seek to return to some of the old systems, which were so damaging, and there are issues of diminishing resources and the instability of the land due to prior mistreatment. While we believe that we have created the most stable structure possible at this time, the future is never certain, and so there are many who find it difficult to maintain an optimistic and peaceful existence.

2. **Purpose** – Our society greatly encourages the discovery and expression of one's individual gifts and talents. As such, it encourages all individuals to discover that which brings them the greatest satisfaction and joy in their life. This discovery comes easily to some, but others find it more difficult and they sometimes struggle with the idea of purpose and passion. There are those whose passion is a singular form of work or talent, and they will pursue that passion throughout their lifetime, but there are others for whom this passion is not as clear, and they will try many different occupations and creative endeavors before they are able to settle into what it is that makes them happiest. And there are still others who struggle with the notion of purpose their whole lives and become frustrated with the notion that they should even have a life's purpose at all. We would say that even the struggle with the notion of purpose is in itself a purpose, as it allows the individual to experience many different forms of self-expression in one lifetime. But often the individual will not view it that way and will desire a more stable sense of purpose that brings them satisfaction and fulfillment.

3. **Status** – Without a monetary system to create a class system and a sense of status through wealth, there are some who desire a different type of status within their community. While there are positions of leadership available to some, there are others who feel cheated out of the ability to reach a high status and so will look for other ways to achieve a sense of importance and a role that earns them some degree of respect. This sometimes causes a conflict of personalities, as these individuals who seek status

are often driven by ego and a need to feel important, rather than expressing a true desire to serve, and it is this type of personality that led us in the direction of a dangerous downfall of our society and its systems. We have found that while we can create new and better systems for the greater good of all, we cannot change the personalities of the individuals within that system, and so it is quite inevitable that conflicts of interest will arise, even in times of peace and abundance. As the notion of status diminishes in favor, these issues also diminish, but they still tend to arise from time to time.

4. **Creative Expression** – As stated previously, this has been found to be one of the best ways to create a form of self-expressive energy—which is needed for the evolution of our species and planet to continue in a positive direction—and so creativity is encouraged among all our inhabitants. Of course, there will be those who exhibit a great deal of creative talent, and some who do not feel that their creativity meets certain standards and so they will be reluctant to try different forms of art, whether it be visual arts or performance. For these individuals, we encourage different forms of self-expression that may not be seen as traditional art forms, such as design, or technology, or storytelling, or botany. But there are still those who will be harsh critics of their own creativity and will be self-conscious in the expression of themselves. Again, this is a problem that is diminishing, but one that we are seeking to eliminate with a broader sense of the definition of creativity.

5. **Happiness through Love** – This, we find, is quite the universal desire, as all beings wish to give and receive love. It is at the core of our beings and

essential to our survival, and its expression is one that dictates much of the activity in our lives. Even with a looser sense of expression of affection and love in our society now, it is still something that many individuals continually seek and struggle with. Relationships are inherently challenging, and it is within those challenges that we are better able to know ourselves. But also within those challenges can be great heartbreak and suffering, and so the heart seeks the purest expression of itself in another despite the struggles inherent in that search. It is our contention that this continual search is a reflection of our desire to connect with Divine Love, and it is this quest that drives us to find that connection with others in our physical lives. As with all societies, there will be some for whom loving relationships come more easily than others, and some who find satisfaction in traditional relationships and some who do not wish to limit themselves in that way. But in all cases, it is a desire to love and be loved that drives us forward in our work, in our social lives, and in our personal relationships.

6. **A More Stable Environment** – As we have stated, we inhabit a planet whose environment can be quite harsh. This creates long periods of time when we must avoid being out in the air, and this can cause some hardship for some who desire the freedom of the outdoors. These individuals find themselves longing for a place where they are able to experience more freedom in the environment and less confinement due to the nature of our planet. There have been scientific speculations about how to create change in the environment of our planet, but none of these come without risks, and so we have

been reluctant to experiment with them. But the dream remains of a planet that affords the pleasant atmosphere similar to that which you enjoy on Earth.

7. **A Deeper Connection to Source through Others** – Those of us who are doing this type of work with other beings in the universe are drawn to it out of a desire to bring them to a deeper connection to the divine within, and in so doing, to deepen our own connection with Source. We seek to fulfill the highest calling of our hearts and the longing of our souls to bring the spiritual experience to the physical, to renew our spiritual essence by bringing knowledge of it to others, to empower ourselves by empowering others. We truly believe that through service to others, we are fulfilling the true calling of this incarnation for ourselves, and that we are doing the highest spiritual work possible while still in the physical. We recognize that there are many in the universe who are called to this work, and it is an aspect of the divine that is the deepest privilege to experience.

8. **A New Home Planet** – There is an aspect of our travels that is research. We are observing other worlds not only with the intention of spreading knowledge and wisdom, but also to observe how other systems work and how they deal with some of the challenges we face in our world. There are many on our planet who feel the time is coming for us to leave our home and inhabit another world that would be compatible to us. While we, as a group, are not convinced that this is the only answer to some of the challenges we are facing with our environment, we are actively seeking alternatives, should that need arise. So far, we have not yet identified a suitable environment for

this type of migration, but we have also not yet ruled it out.

9. **A Deeper Understanding of Universal Laws –** We have learned much through the challenges of our planet and the transformation of our systems, which reflect the aspects of divine connection and expression, and yet we know that there is still much to be learned. As we observe the evolution of our own species and planet, in addition to that of other worlds, we are more and more aware of the interconnectedness of all species, all systems, and all worlds through an intricate energetic web of experience and energy. The complexity of these connections is quite fascinating, and there are many aspects of it that we still do not understand. While we know that there will always be some facets of the divine plan that will forever remain beyond our scope of understanding, we feel drawn to continue our research and our exploration so that we can better understand these connections and use that understanding to bring a greater sense of oneness, peace, and self-knowledge to all we encounter.

10. **Beauty –** As it is in your culture, we are drawn to that which we find beautiful, and while our personal ideas of beauty will vary greatly, there are certain characteristics of beauty that are universal and that may impart a greater sense of the divine, which is present in all things. While you may find the appearance of our planet rather dull and bleak compared to the richness of your own, we are conditioned to find beauty in even the most mundane aspects of existence, and we are intrinsically drawn to observe beauty in all its many forms. It is an interesting phenomenon to observe,

that those who are surrounded by the beauty of rich diversity and incredible color and form will tend to begin to take these things for granted and will not, as a rule, seek beauty as inspiration in their lives, while those who have less in the way of traditional forms of beauty surrounding them will find great pleasure in seeking it out and discovering it. And so it is with a sense of wonder and delight that we observe the incredible richness of beauty in the universe, and find evidence of the divine presence in all that we find pleasing, especially in those things that may not fit the universal ideals of that which is called beautiful.

WHAT ARE THE TOP 10 MYSTERIES YOU FACE—PHYSICAL, SPIRITUAL, PSYCHOLOGICAL, OR OTHERWISE?

1. **Our Origins** – We do not have the wealth of information that you have available in your world to explain the evolution of our species or how we came to be on our planet. There is very little evidence of our ancestors, and there are stories passed down through the generations about another world where those who came before us lived. We believe that our species migrated from elsewhere in the universe at some point, but we do not have any hard evidence of where we originated or exactly when or how this migration occurred. There are aspects of our physiology that suggest that we were once more adapted to a semi-aquatic life, but this is not the nature of our planet now.

2. **The Origins of Others** – We have encountered many different species of beings in the universe, and

while there is much speculation about how these
different species evolved, there are always points in
that evolution where the information is not so clear
and there are gaps in the evidence. We see this in
your own species, and your scientists will tend to fill
these gaps with hypotheses that come to be accepted
as facts, when in actuality these facts are simply
educated guesses. We are unsure how some species
came to be, and what forces caused them to evolve in
the way that they did, despite a vast accumulation of
knowledge about the universe.

3. **The Origin of Our Planet** – There is evidence
    that our planet was once a part of a much larger
    body that broke off in some type of cosmic collision
    or explosive event. Various forms of space debris
    point to a huge event in our solar system that
    altered the structure of many cosmic bodies and
    created new planets such as ours. Scientists believe
    that the original planet had a much less hostile
    environment, as its orbit was farther away from our
    stars, and so there is speculation that there may have
    been some similarities to your Earth in the original
    atmosphere of this much larger cosmic body. We
    are unsure if there were conscious life-forms on this
    original planet, as there is nothing remaining of it.
    Some forms of scientific inquiry that involve what
    you would call remote viewing through time have
    suggested that the original planet was quite lush with
    many life-forms, but that these were obliterated in
    some type of cosmic catastrophe.

4. **The Hardiness of Some Plants** – There are
    certain plant forms on our planet that defy the
    laws of physics in the manner in which they are

able to thrive and propagate in the environmental conditions of our world—and yet they do. They seem to have evolved some intricate systems that have allowed them to maintain life on an atomic level even when the plant appears to be dead, and those atomic structures of life will be enough to regenerate the plant when the conditions are more suitable. It is a fascinating and mysterious process that has baffled those who have studied it.

5. **Altered DNA Structure** – As your scientists know, DNA is the building block of all life-forms, and it is the same type of structure that determines the characteristics of the beings on our planet. As it is studied, the genetic code of the DNA of the children of certain individuals should contain certain aspects that correspond to that of the biological parents. We have found, however, that in an increasing number, the DNA structure of our offspring corresponds less and less to that of its birth parents. The studies done on this type of anomaly indicate that there is an evolution occurring in our species that is not necessarily obvious in the genetic code of the parents of the offspring who are exhibiting these new types of DNA code. It is as though these beings were genetically programmed to mutate at this particular time, in accordance with the environmental and physical structure of our world. We will continue to study this at length, but so far we have been unable to pinpoint the nature of this shift and how it is programmed into the structure of the DNA.

6. **Life on Other Worlds** – In our nonphysical travels throughout the universe, we have encountered physical structures on some planets that have the

appearance of being constructed by intelligent life-forms, but there did not appear to be any of these life-forms present at the time of our visit. We are unsure of what happened to these beings. It could be that they succumbed to harsh conditions or perhaps some sort of cosmic event, but on several occasions we were unable to discern any conscious life on many of these planets.

7. **Forces of the Universe** – There are some forces in the universe that are as yet undefined and unlabeled by your scientists but that we have discovered as key components to the operation of the galactic bodies and the orbit of the celestial bodies both in your universe and ours. These forces seem to operate independently of gravity and magnetic alignment, and create motion and expansion without the rules that we would normally expect to find in play. We have identified many more forces than were previously thought to exist, but there are still many mysteries in the universe that keep our scientists and researchers busy.

8. **Spirit Consciousness** – As we travel throughout the universe as a form of spirit energy, we encounter other beings in spirit form. Many are spirit forms that we can identify as nonphysical beings, either from life-forms that have left the physical plane, or other higher forms of beings. But there are others that we have not been able to identify as anything we have previously identified or named. These beings sometimes seem to emanate from the physical world, and others seem to be beings who have not incarnated in the fashion we are used to seeing. These beings all appear to serve an important purpose in

the balance of energy throughout the cosmos, and
their energy is quite fascinating to us.

9. **Our Vision** – There appears to be some sort of
    genetic or environmental mutation occurring in the
    vision of many of our inhabitants. These individuals
    are finding that the way they perceive their
    environment visually is shifting, and that their color,
    light, and depth perception are being altered. This
    is quite a new phenomenon, and one that is causing
    some discomfort with those who first encounter it;
    however, they find that once they are able to adapt to
    it, it reveals some aspects of our world that were not
    previously available to our senses. We believe there is
    some type of environmental shift causing this, but it
    has not yet been identified.

10. **You** – We find your species to be quite fascinating
    and we are extremely fond of you. There are many
    aspects of your experience that we do not fully
    understand but that we find quite pleasing. We are
    emotional beings, but the incredible diversity of
    emotion that one of your beings is able to experience
    in just a short period of time is quite amazing to us.
    We are also fascinated by the ability of some of your
    species to be so good at the art of deception; in fact,
    we find that this trait is quite a common one on your
    planet, and that many rarely speak what they are
    truly feeling or experiencing as truth. This is not to
    say that our species does not have those with similar
    inclinations, but we are quite amazed (and amused)
    by the great lengths some of your species will go to
    perpetuate an untruth.

PART 2

LIFE
ON
EARTH

My questions in this section are to
probe what Frank knows about who
we are and where we've been, as well
as to learn from them as much as
possible about our history and place
in creation that we've not yet learned
from our own discoveries
and self-reflection.

HOW MANY CIVILIZATIONS ON EARTH HAVE YOU WITNESSED?

In the unlimited spirit aspect of our beings, we have been able to witness many historical events on your planet, and it is through the understanding of your planet's evolution that we have been motivated to step in and express our perspective on the direction that you are heading and what could be done to improve that trajectory. There have been many in your history who have understood the great power that could be harnessed through the manipulation of energy. This is evident in the pyramid structures and other megalithic structures around your world. The aspect of mystery surrounding these objects is quite deliberate, as it is mystery that prompts exploration and discovery. Without some sort of unknown, there is a sense of stagnation and a ceasing of wonder. These are deadly to any system, and so we ask that you always maintain a certain amount of awe and wonder in the amazing world around you.

WHAT HAPPENED TO EARTH'S EARLIER CIVILIZATIONS, OF WHICH WE NOW SEE ANCIENT AND OFTEN MYSTERIOUS RUINS THAT LITTER THE GLOBE?

Understand that there is a constant ebb and flow of energetic expressions of Source energy within the universe, and that these expressions can take the form of physical beings of many different levels of advancement. Within these levels will be anything from plant life and simple creatures to highly intelligent, spiritually advanced beings of many different forms. Each of these beings is a divine aspect of the Source energy from which it originates, and each has its own form of expression and influence on all other beings around it; as such, these highly advanced creatures serve no greater purpose than that of a tree or a flowering bush. This is not to say that they are on the same energetic level, but that their purpose is not necessarily a greater one.

And so, as you look upon the forces of nature and the many different forms of consciousness within it, you will see that these life-forms continue to experience some sort of evolution, some sort of transmutation, and some sort of change within the web of conscious creation, and it is that continual energetic evolution that animates the nature of reality. Within that evolution will sometimes be a loss of that type of being, which you will call extinction when it comes to plants and animals that no longer exist in your energetic field of reality. However, as you know, there is no loss of energy; that is not possible, and so it is through that extinction that new life-forms can emerge and new expressions of Source will make themselves known. It is the progression that led to the emergence of your species and all others.

And so, each of the advanced civilizations that emerged at various times upon your planet existed to serve a certain purpose in the evolution of your world, and their disappearance also has served to allow other forms of energetic expression to emerge. Those beings have not disappeared, any more than any spiritual being could; they have found other ways to express their energetic powers of creation through different types of physical and spiritual incarnations, and the impact of their existence continues to be felt on your planet today. As such, no physical expression of Source is wasted, lost, or without purpose, and the energetic aspect of those beings lives on in other ways.

Remember that no being can have its life taken away from it without its consent on a soul level. And so, these civilizations agreed to have brief and very powerful appearances in the physical realm and you can be sure that they did so gladly and with reverence for the experience. Every being leaves its mark, and these civilizations made it possible for your life to be the way it is in the present moment.

But where did these advanced civilizations come from and where did they go? Did each evolve upon the ruins of the one before it? Did all the earlier ones collapse? How many might we be talking—4, 40, 400?

Within this question is a great multitude of questions that would involve many pages of text to answer, and so we will address it here as succinctly as possible. Within the evolution of your species lie many different mutations involving the genetic structure and intellectual capacity of the various genera of species. The idea that there was one steady stream of evolution from one species to the next is not necessarily true, although there have been many genetic mutations occurring naturally in the way the human being has developed into the species that inhabits your planet at this time.

To address the question of their origin, one must consider the origin of all human species on your planet and, in fact, all living beings in the universe. There are many energetic effects at play here, when it comes to the emergence of a species or genus of creature, of which evolution is only one method, and quite an unreliable one at that. Suffice to say that the idea of creation being spurred by desire, by thought, and through love is quite correct, and while the origin of these creative forces is always Source, the methods used vary widely. As with most hypotheses and conjectures, there is a certain level of truth present; the thought that there has been otherworldly intervention, that the sudden mutation of genetic materials has occurred as a result of some supernatural force, and that there has been crossbreeding of human and alien life has a certain amount of truth to it, but it is not quite as easily explained as that. We could quite certainly fill the pages of an entire volume with what we know about this and still not create an accurate picture of the truth.

We simply would like you to know that these "advanced civilizations" emerged just as you did, as an extension of Source energy, with the intention of bringing to the physical existence an aspect of Source and as an experiment of sorts, which is the way Source manifests its infinite variety of energetic components into what you know as reality.

Therefore, if you think of these civilizations as theater performers, if you see them as fulfilling a certain role in the overall evolution of your physical existence, and if you see yourselves as the same, it is a natural part of that evolution that some expressions of Source will live out their purpose in a short period of time and others will find their purpose extends into a longer time period. These civilizations had their place, but they were not sustainable for a multitude of reasons. One of the most outstanding reasons is that they reached the limit of their evolutionary progress; that is to say, they reached a point in their societies where any further advancements would be beyond the limitations of the Earth's evolution at that period in time. There simply weren't enough resources available or general technological or manufacturing advancements available to meet the demands of their intellectual capacity.

What is evident from this is that a harmonic existence must be present between the general evolutionary progress of the Earth itself, its various creatures, and its human civilizations in order for there to be a continuation of any species. The extinctions you are now seeing among the species on your planet are due to a sense of disharmony with their existence and the nature of your Earth and its human inhabitants. As these extinctions progress, you will also witness the evolution of new species that are better able to survive the very challenging nature of your planet.

It is vital that you understand that every creature's energetic contribution to the planet is vital, but also that as the Earth shifts and changes, these energetic forces and needs too will shift and change, and so you will find that certain species no longer resonate with the energetic footprint of your world. While this creates a sense of tragic loss, it is inevitable that these shifts and changes will continue to occur. By all means, continue your ecological work to preserve all the species you can, but also be aware that the natural evolution of your planet contains a need for loss just as it contains a need for new energetic expressions.

Each advanced civilization left a huge energetic impact on the evolution of your Earth and on your species. Your current world would not be what it is without them, and the same can be said for yourselves. There is no life or death without purpose. As such, each subsequent civilization has, in effect, built itself up from the ruins of the last, but not quite in such an obvious way. Just as you come into this incarnation with no memory of your origin, your species come into consciousness without a memory of those that came before them, for the express purpose of experiencing their lives from the perspective of discovery and wonder.

There have been many hundreds of different civilizations that have existed on your planet. Rest assured that your investigations have unearthed merely a fraction of them.

WHAT CAN YOU SHARE WITH US ABOUT WHO CREATED THE FAMOUS PYRAMIDS ON THE GIZA PLATEAU IN TODAY'S EGYPT— WHY THEY WERE BUILT, HOW THEY WERE BUILT, AND WHAT WE MAY STILL LEARN FROM THEM? AND—IF YOU WOULD—WAS THE GREAT SPHINX OF GIZA PART OF THE PYRAMID COMPLEX OR ENTIRELY DIFFERENT? IF DIFFERENT, WHY WAS IT BUILT AND BY WHOM?

This is quite a complicated issue that would require many pages of explanation; suffice to say that many seemingly miraculous things are accomplished through sheer will and ingenuity. You are witnessing this every day, so do not discount the power of the human mind by assuming some supernatural intervention. The human mind has its own type of supernatural abilities when properly motivated.

WHAT DO YOU KNOW OF OUR BIGFOOT, FAIRIES, LEPRECHAUNS, LOCH NESS MONSTER, CHUPACABRAS, AND SO ON?

There are many mysteries in your world that are perpetuated by myth, fear, and a love for the unknown. Some are based on fact and others are pure fantasy, but that does not negate their powerful presence in the lore of your planet. We are aware of tremendous sea creatures that reside in the great depths of your bodies of water and it is true that these creatures continue to exist in some form; however, we do not feel that the depiction of these creatures is generally accurate. The beast in the depths of the Loch in Scotland is simply a gentle serpent of which there are several still living in its great depths. And so this creature is simply a remainder from your prehistoric times and is a physical being. There have been other beings that are genetic mutations of animals that have been mistaken for mythical creatures, such as the Yeti and ape-like creature known as Bigfoot. However, many of the sightings of these creatures have been fabricated to perpetuate the myth and mystery. Still other experiences are deliberately masked visitations of otherworldly creatures who come to study your planet. Many of these creatures have the ability to alter the perception of the experience so that they are perceived as a mysterious earthly mutation rather than a creature from another world. This is not done with the intention to harm or frighten but merely to allow them to continue their study without the risk of capture or mass fear. No visitors to your planet come with the intention of harm; however, their understanding of your emotions of fear and terror can be quite limited. Beings such as fairies are certain forms of elemental spirits that exist solely in the form of nonmaterial energy, but which can be perceived by certain individuals under the right circumstances. There are many types of spirit beings that exist in the universe with different trajectories of experience far removed from the material existence experienced by yourselves and ourselves. The universe teems with this energetic force, and it is all connected to Source and is all part of the infinite expression of that Source energy. Much of this energy defies description and yet we attempt to label and define it, as it is in our very nature to do so. We suggest that you see this energy as one of the great wonders of the universe and evidence of the infinite creative power of Source energy.

ARE WE MORE OR LESS PRIMITIVE THAN OTHER WORLDS?

We do not view your world as primitive; in fact, we are immensely impressed with the progress your people continue to make in such a limited amount of universal time. We understand the struggle of what appears to be the minority to create change when it is met with the social brainwashing of those who hold power and have become corrupted by it. However, we want to assure you that it is this desire for change that will triumph over the misguided paths and limited vision of those who appear to be the gatekeepers. Their power is ephemeral; it is as mythical as some of those creatures mentioned above, and it will not prevail over the determination of those whose motivation is clear and pure. We are quite touched and moved by the emotional intensity of those of you who strive to create change not only in your own lives but in the energetic field of your planet. This is not the work of a primitive people; in fact, the imbalance that exists is solely due to the vast acceleration of consciousness being met with a somewhat primitive social structure that rewards greed and the misuse of power. We have witnessed the swift destruction of other forms of civilization in the universe; but know that no form of life is ever completely annihilated, as it continues to evolve in a nonmaterial way to assist in the evolution of the universal energy back to Source.

CAN YOU SPECIFICALLY SPEAK TO THE ORIGINS AND DEMISE OF ATLANTIS? WAS IT THE "GREATEST" (LARGEST, LONGEST-RUNNING, MOST ADVANCED) OF ALL EARLIER CIVILIZATIONS?

We find no benefit in comparing the worth of the many civilizations that have inhabited your planet, as each has contributed greatly to the overall evolution and progress of it. Atlantis is merely one that has received a lot of attention among those who investigate these things in your world, and as such, its importance is inflated. In the grand scheme of the universe, its longevity was relatively short, its impact relatively powerful, and its life expression equal to your own.

IT IS SAID THAT THE ATLANTEANS KNEW HOW TO HARNESS POWER FROM CRYSTALS; IS THIS TRUE? ARE THE CRYSTALS WE FIND HERE ON EARTH LIKE THE ONES THAT EMANATE POWER ON YOUR PLANET? HOW CAN WE HARNESS CRYSTAL POWER? IS IT THROUGH THOUGHT? AND/OR IS MERELY HOLDING OR WEARING THE CRYSTALS USEFUL?

It is true that those from the continent of Atlantis were able to harness energy from crystals and other methods that were more focused on the natural energetic fields available to all. The energetic forces of crystals are understood by some of your scientists but these findings are disclosed in only a limited way. There is a combination of factors here that is preventing the disclosure of crystal-based energy; suffice it to say that there is much to be learned about the power of substances produced by your earth that are renewable and less destructive to the environment than fossil fuels.

The crystals found within your earth are similar in structure and composition to those found on our planet, and in fact, there are many similarities in the energetic structure of planetary materials among all the planets in the universe. Just as no individual entity is exactly like another, crystals will have many qualities that are unique and many that are the same, depending on the environmental factors that created them. But all wield different types of energetic power that can be harnessed in various ways. Using crystals to produce enough energy to power the vast number of devices used in your world is possible, but the combination of factors needed for this to occur has not yet been mass-produced. This is not due to a lack of knowledge; rather, it is through a suppression of information and the power of corporate entities that monopolize the research in this field.

Crystal energy can be harnessed with a combination of solar energy and the geometric structure of the crystalline molecules that magnify the power of that light energy. There are certain types of crystals that are most suited for this, and some can be used in combination with others for a more powerful result. While those we have available on our planet vary from the crystals you have discovered on yours, it is our contention that the same results could be obtained with those you have available at this time, and that certain physicists and scientists have already produced great results through experimentation in this field. We believe that you will find this information will eventually be disclosed as part of the conscious shift your planet is now experiencing as more and more people demand it.

Working with crystals is a good way to enhance and clear your own energetic field, and so we encourage you to explore this field if it resonates with you. The power of crystals has long been known in your culture, but not always believed. If you are drawn to acquire and work with them, you will find that they can produce results that are quite remarkable, simply by carrying them or placing them in your environment.

CAN YOU GIVE US TIPS ON HOW TO HARNESS OTHER UNIVERSAL ENERGIES—PARTICULARLY THOSE THAT ARE EASIEST TO ACCESS?

The most accessible universal energies are those that are already present within you. And yet, these energies are often the ones that are least utilized due to cultural conditioning that encourages doubt in them. The energy of your thoughts is an excellent example of this, and this is something that is widely examined and stressed in the teachings of your own work, Mike. We would like you to apply these same principles to understanding and seeking all other types of energy that may be available but not widely utilized due to a structure of belief prevalent on Earth that is contrary to them. As with all change, first work on the self, and in harnessing your own miraculous energy, you will then find the ways to access that which is outside of yourself.

And so, as an energetic being with unlimited powers of creation, one must go within, examine one's belief system about one's own power, and find evidential proof of it. What have you manifested through the power of your thoughts already? There is much evidence of this available to you. How can you take this further? How can you utilize the power of your emotions, your words, and your actions in order to create an energetic flow that is in harmony with all you desire? All of these things are covered in the works of our dear questioner here, and so we will not reiterate them. Instead, we will encourage all who read these words to put them into practice on a regular basis. *This* is how you will begin to harness the most miraculous energy available to you.

From there, it is a matter of applying the same principles to other forms of energy. The energy of the sun is already widely used and the use of this type of renewable energy is increasing as the population sees the benefits of it. The power of the wind is much the same, and experimentation is being done with expanding the use of the power of water.

Some other types of energy that have not yet been examined in your culture include the energy of heat and cold, the energy of concentrated thought, and the energy of growing things such as plant life. Magnetic energy has had some attention but its full potential is not yet realized on your planet, nor has the energy of gravity and the orbits of the planets in your solar system.

While we will not begin to explain these in scientific terms, we can assure you that there is much more to be discovered, expanded upon, and learned in the field of energetic study, but only when the threshold of belief is crossed and the limitations of the vested interests of corporate funding are overcome. You have only just begun to scratch the surface of what is possible with what is already available to you.

MIGHT YOU EXPLAIN YOUR REFERENCE TO THE "ENERGY OF CONCENTRATED THOUGHT"? WHAT DO YOU MEAN BY THAT, HOW IS IT CREATED, AND HOW CAN WE HARNESS IT?

This power has been demonstrated numerous times by various yogis and others who have perfected the art of meditation and deliberate conscious manipulation of the body's energy. It is the same technique that is used for energetic healing, focused energetic connection with others, and other phenomena such as psychokinesis and thought transference. It is achieved through practiced focus and relaxation, and it is what allows many to experience a heightened connection with themselves as higher beings and with other forms of existence, both in the physical and in pure energy.

Your science has only begun to comprehend what can be accomplished through the power of the energetic mind, and there is much to be learned from the spiritual masters who already practice these things.

HOW MUCH MORE CAN WE ASPIRE TO IN TERMS OF SPIRITUAL EVOLUTION?

Spiritual evolution, as an expression of Source, is unlimited. The experience of a material life, wherever and however this is achieved, is merely a small and sacred part of your spiritual existence. You are a multidimensional being simultaneously expressing itself through multiple forms of existence, each one affording vast opportunity for knowledge and understanding. Even those who do not appear to evolve within this lifetime experience a huge shift through the experience of material life once they return to their spiritual source. No life is without that opportunity and no spirit experiences a material lifetime in vain. The infinite nature of the energetic universe is a difficult concept for those experiencing a physical life to grasp, and in fact, we ourselves do not fully comprehend it, although we have felt it and it is an immensely satisfying experience.

ARE YOU AWARE OF ANY IMPENDING CONTACT WITH ALIENS AND EARTHLINGS, PHYSICALLY?

This contact has occurred and continues with regular frequency. However, there is such a social stigma surrounding the perception of these experiences that those who report them are often labeled as mentally unstable or liars. Still others have their perception altered and are left with only a vague notion of an unusual experience. There is an understanding among the visitors to your planet that their discovery would not bode well for them, and so they employ any means available to avoid detection. At the same time, they continue to gain knowledge of the universe through the study of your rich and varied landscapes. Open contact with other worlds will not be achieved until the systems in place are changed to ones that are open to that connection and will not perceive it as a threat. Clearly, your civilization as a whole is not quite ready yet. Those who have experienced contact are often quite disturbed by it; Tracy has been associated with one who has had this type of experience. Until the concepts of universal energy are understood and other life-forms are seen to be just as sacred as your own, these experiences will be interpreted in a negative way and will not be generally supported and accepted.

WHEN WE HAVE DONE WHAT WE CHOSE THIS LIFETIME TO DO, IS IT POSSIBLE TO RAISE OUR VIBRATION AND DISAPPEAR, RATHER THAN PHYSICALLY DIE?

That concept is not far from the truth of death in the material sense. It is simply a separation of the spiritual essence from the physical body, which will in a sense disappear. The spiritual essence does not alter, fade, or die, but all material things eventually do, and this is one of the great opportunities for spiritual advancement while still in the physical; the acceptance of the death experience as a sacred part of life, rather than as a tragic ending, is one of the most transformative steps toward spiritual evolution in any civilization. And so even those who achieve the highest elevation of vibrational frequency while still in the physical will have to experience death in the conventional sense, since it is part of the universal evolutionary process.

WHAT IS YOUR BEST ADVICE FoR HUMANS TO LIVE HEALTHIER LIVES?

Balance is the key to a physically healthy existence. Returning to a more earth-based existence is beneficial, but that does not mean that all scientific advances made in the field of nutrition need to be negated. Awareness of the body's cycles and rhythms is extremely beneficial, but this needs to be done on an individual path, as the individual frequency of each being must be taken into account. The fields of nutrition and medicine often overlook the vibrational frequency of each being and instead group issues of health and wellness in categories that dictate the modes of treatment based on the disease rather than the individual. It is vastly important for each individual to gauge their own sense of wellness and to become acutely involved in their own well-being and the rhythms and cycles of their own bodies. While it is true that great strides have been made within your fields of medicine and wellness, there have also been huge shifts into modes of disease that perpetuate themselves through fear and reliance on the medical community. The diagnosis often creates the disease, and the fear of death often blocks healing and recovery. All forms of energetic wellness can be successfully integrated into conventional forms of medicine to create a holistic practice that supports healing rather than promoting disease. You are your own best physician; become aware of your own power to energetically heal and support your own physical system.

IN AN EARLIER EXCHANGE, YOU SHARED THAT THERe NOW
EXISTS, ON EARTH, THE BEGINnINGS OF A CURE FoR CYSTIC
fiBROSIS THAT'S BEeN COVEReD UP oR STALIED BY CoRPoRATE
PROfiT—SEeKING. CAN YOU PLEASE EXPOUND?

Within the fields of medicine and science, there are an
equal number of answers and questions; just as one question is
answered, another question emerges, and this is part of the evolution of understanding that is in a constant state of flux. Just as
your desires spur action and purpose, the challenges facing the
physical experience lead to the action of purpose of finding the
answers and cures. This is the natural flow of existence, and it is
what creates the energetic flow of being that engages your energy
with one another and the community you belong to.

There are, however, aspects of physical existence that resist
finding answers, as the unanswered questions create need, and
that need fulfills greed. And so, within a needy society there are
pockets to be filled. This is not to say that the majority of medical and scientific researchers are motivated by this greed, but it is
true that they are financed by it, and this creates an atmosphere
of holding individuals in the energy of sickness so that they can
be dependent upon the products that are created as a measure of
relief for them, but not necessarily a cure.

The genetic disposition of the disease of cystic fibrosis is
already understood. There have been very successful experiments
with human subjects using mutated genes that form a sort of
chain reaction within the organism to relieve the overproduction
of diseased cells and create a new generation of healthy ones. But
as there is a business built around the treatment and systematic
support of the disease, and not necessarily support of the patient,
there is little funding available for what are being touted as experi-
mental or not scientifically proven methods.

You can be sure, though, that with the persistent will of those
who are determined to advance these cures, the treatments will
not be cloaked for long, and the methods will soon become more
public. This will lead to more public demand and a greater outcry

against the greed that keeps them hidden. It is the same for other high-risk diseases that have generated a huge range of manufactured pharmaceuticals and treatments that serve only to relieve symptoms, but not necessarily effect a cure.

Those who choose to bring these diseases into the world through their physical incarnations have done so with the full knowledge of the challenges they will incur, and they are here to bring knowledge and awareness of the nature of compassion, health, and greed to the forefront so that these systems can be healed.[2]

SPEAK TO INTELLIGENCE (EMOTIONAL AND INTELLECTUAL); IT SEEMS SO LACKING IN MANY PEOPLE. ARE WE JUST LAZY IN THOUGHT?

We would suggest that you broaden your definition of intelligence, as we have found that the limitations placed on this concept often negate intrinsic forms of knowledge that are just as vital to your life experience as others. The traditional ideas around intelligence are quite narrow; they consist of conventional learning and education, rule-following, and constrained ideas about the nature of your world and the universe. Those who do not value this type of knowledge are not necessarily lacking in intelligence; in fact, their purpose may be to broaden *your* view of the world to include a more visceral sense of knowledge such as forms of social communication and a deeper sense of connection without the constraints of conventional knowledge. Those who appear to be of a lower state of consciousness are experiencing the world in a very deliberate way; it is their divine path and it is vital to their own experience and that of the world in general. One cannot

---

2   Author's Note: This is not meant to be an indictment on any organization or field, nor have we asked Frank for any follow-up information, as we know too well that they're not the sort to divulge more than is necessary to inspire our own inner and outer searching.

dictate the value of experience by confining it to the narrow space of conventional education and knowledge. There are many layers of conscious expression and they are all quite valuable, whether they are expressions of conventional intelligence, emotional expression, communication of the heart, or simply a sense of being present in the world without the higher brain functions that are valued and emphasized in your culture. Universal intelligence is far greater than any form of brain function, and it is where we return when we are released from the physical constraints of that brain. The concept of laziness is one that is more closely linked with a disconnection from the higher forms of consciousness that urge us on toward a higher expression of ourselves. It is through the social conditioning of the masses that this type of apathy becomes laziness, and it is through the realization and exploration of ourselves as higher beings that we are propelled out of that sense of complacency, and not necessarily toward an emphasis on brain-centered intelligence.

I'VE NOTICED IN A VERY FEW PEOPLE THE SEeMINGLY UNIQUE ABILITY TO ENHANCE THEIR OWN INTELlIGENCE TO LEVeLS WELl BEYOND THAT WITH WHICH THEY WERe BoRN, ADdING GREATLY TO THEIR QUALITY OF LIFE. FoR MOST PEOPLE, THOUGH, THIS ABILITY SEeMS COMPLETeLY ABSENT, FoR WHICH THEY'RE COM-PARaTIVELY HANDICAPpED. WHAT IS THIS ABILITY? IS IT WISDOM oR "STREeT SMARTS"? IS IT EARNED? IS IT A PSYCHIC PHENOM-ENON? IS IT A CHOSEN DISPENSATION?

The intelligence that you speak of is not what we would consider intelligence at all; it is an awareness of one's own power of discernment, one's own connection with Divine Intelligence, and one's inner wisdom, which all have unlimited potential to answer, assist, and guide. It is true that this type of awareness is rare, although we find that it is a growing phenomenon on your planet that is connected to the shift of consciousness occurring in the present time.

This type of awareness is strongest in those who have done the inner exploration that has led them to a greater understanding of themselves as an extension of divine energy, not a separate entity from it. This is not an easy concept for many to grasp, and even among those who believe they have grasped it is the stubborn will that holds on to aspects of the old belief systems that can help the individual feel safe, less responsible for their own lives, and comfortably ignorant. There is a sense that this behavior is often rewarded in your culture; "intelligence" of this nature is not often seen as a benefit except among those who possess it and practice it. To those who avoid the desire to cultivate it, it seems like a waste of time, as the ability to coast through life appears to be much less work. Again, this can stem from the sense of laziness that we discussed earlier, but it more likely comes from a long-standing belief system that dictates that humans are victims of a life they didn't ask for, in a world that is flawed, among people who are constant challenges, and with insurmountable difficulties such as health issues, relationship issues, and work issues. Although it does not create much happiness in the individual, this type of unconscious coasting through life helps people feel that they are off the hook, that they no longer have to take on any more responsibilities to themselves, and that they can continue to rely on others to either solve their problems or support them with sympathy.

All beings are born with the spark of the divine within them; however, not all beings choose an incarnation in which they are conscious of this spark and can delve more deeply into it. This is by design; these beings who appear to be sleepwalking are vital to the balance of the social structure on your planet; there cannot be Divine Intelligence without ignorance, just as there cannot be enlightenment without unconsciousness. Those who choose the less conscious state are not choosing badly; they are providing valuable insights to those around them who contemplate questions such as the one you've asked here. They represent a different perspective on the world, which may seem childish or ridiculous to those who are more grounded in the truth and more connected to the inner spirit. However, their very ignorance may motivate others to explore their own awareness and intelligence, and ask the deeper questions of themselves and those around them. In other words, when we are presented with that which reflects poorly on us, we have the option to delve more deeply within, rather than concern ourselves too much with dwelling on the problems and issues of others.

While these people will challenge you, and perhaps even hinder some of your growth through their excessive time-wasting tactics, please know that your work has a deep and profound effect on ALL beings, even those who are having a difficult time assimilating it. There is an energy to the word written with a deep sense of truth and love that will resonate even among those who have never opened one of your books, Mike, or have never delved more deeply into the mysteries of the universe than their own front yard. These beings provide lightworkers such as yourself with a mission. They are the ones who have not yet been reached with the truth; in fact, they may never be reached in this lifetime, but that just means their life path is designed for some other purpose that is just as grand.

It is also important to note that in the work that you are so graciously doing in the world, you are attracting scores of people who are looking outside of themselves for truth because they are blind to the truths that lie within. This means that your daily experience is filled with evidence of this lack of awareness or intelligence, and so your perception is that the world is hopelessly filled with these types of people. In truth, there are many present in your world who are moving beyond ignorance every day, and who are exploring more deeply—and more universally—the idea of truth and the meaning of all that they experience. Do not despair in your perspective, as it is limited at this time. Instead, focus your attention on those who are seeking to spread the sense of enlightenment to everyone, even to those who have created a bit of a mess. These others serve to highlight areas where this work is still needed.

ARE THERE OTHER SPECIES ON EARTH THAT ARE PHILOSOPHI-
CAL? ARE THERE SPECIES THAT WONDER ABOUT HOW THEY
CAME TO BE? IF SO, WHICH TYPES OF ANIMALS/SPECIES? HAVE
YOU HAD A TWO-WAY COmMUNICATION WITH ANY OF THEM?

There are many different levels of intelligence among the sentient beings in your world, and this intelligence does not always
correspond with the ideas you may already have in your belief system about the nature of intelligence. All beings, from the simplest
and smallest to the most complex, have a level of conscious intelligence and awareness of their own existence that goes beyond the
programming of the brain. They are born with an innate knowledge of the nature of being, and for some this knowledge is not
questioned or pondered but simply accepted as the reality of existence. While there is knowledge of past experiences and anticipation of future events, most of these creatures live very much in
the present moment, adjusting their actions to their needs in that
moment and holding their energetic field in whatever that experience is offering them.

As such, most of the creatures you keep as pets are supreme
teachers of the importance and value of this moment-to-moment
experience. It is why you are so innately drawn to the energy of
these creatures, as they do not sit in a sense of regret, or worry, or
judgment. Most of these creatures who are well loved and treated
with respect and caring will exhibit an energy of pure gratitude
and bliss; however, they will also respond emotionally to that
which challenges them, and in that way you are able to relate
and sympathize with these creatures as fellow conscious, feeling beings. You recognize in them an aspect of yourselves that is
sometimes buried beneath the responsibilities you have taken on
and the belief that you need to control your life and environment
at all times. These creatures do not experience such a powerful
need to control; while they have an instinct for survival, which
will often dictate their actions, they will also understand when
they need to simply accept and flow with the experiences that

come their way, and while they can experience sadness, they do not dwell in an energy of regret or self-abasement.

There are some species of creatures on your planet that resonate with higher divine energy and therefore have the capacity of self-awareness on a different level of frequency than others. These creatures have the energetic power of discernment and are more aware of their own free will and connection. We have experienced this in the dolphins and whales, in the higher primates such as gorillas, in elephants, and in some species of parrots. There may be others with this energetic connection that we are not yet aware of, but these are the beings we most recognize as bearing the awareness that gives them a more complex connection to themselves and others. This does not mean that they have the same types of thought processes as humans; there are similarities, but there are also many differences. And so, it is important to understand that they are separate, whole, and complete beings of light in and of themselves, and that the similarities or differences in the consciousness of any being does not make them any more or less valuable to the collective conscious energy of your planet.

We have observed a complex system of thoughts, beliefs, and understanding in the species of creatures we have mentioned, which brings a higher level of awareness to the nature of their being and their influence on their environment and the creatures around them. They have excellent problem-solving skills and are able to change their beliefs when they find it in harmony with their greater good to do so. They can overcome their innate fears in favor of curiosity and the desire to learn and evolve, and they have an awareness of this as an important aspect of their existence. They do not define the nature of a higher power, but they have a sense of the connection with it, and they will be aware of this energy as being a supreme sense of the source of their being. As such, they do not necessarily question this or ponder it as humans do; they simply accept it as part of their existence.

The higher awareness in these creatures leads them into actions that go beyond the simple instinct toward survival, and as such, you may find situations where these creatures will sacrifice themselves in favor of the greater good of the collective. They do not suffer the fear of death quite so much as humans, as they have a higher awareness of death as part of the natural life cycle, and so even though they have a will to live, they also have a natural understanding of the need to die, and sometimes will choose death when it appears to be beneficial to others of their species. This involves a complex thought process that is not available to most other species of being.

These creatures feel a kinship with humans, although they also have an innate fear of them, unless they have been raised to trust them. Even those who naturally fear humans can feel that kinship and will use their natural instincts and intuition to guide them to seek out humans if they need help or rescue. This applies to the less complex consciousness of other species, as well. There is a sense of kinship in many creatures with one another and with the energy of humans, and so even for those creatures who will defend themselves in what is perceived to be a violent way, or who may hunt a human as a food source, there is an awareness of the higher consciousness of humans and a form of respect for that consciousness, which can manifest as fear or as curiosity, depending on the circumstances.

And so, there is much to be learned from all the creatures on your planet, both those who have what you would deem a lower form of consciousness and those who have complex structures of intellect, awareness, and emotions. They are all related to you in their physical nature, their energetic nature, and the energy of their spirits, and in this way they all deserve your respect, compassion, and loving care. We would suggest that you look at them in wonder and awe, and ask them what they have to teach you when they appear in your lives, as even those who do not exhibit higher consciousness are directly connected to Source, and as aspects of divine energy that are different from that which you experience in your own existence, they have much to show you about the nature of reality.

CAN YOU PLEASE SPEAK TO THE POLARIZATION WE TEND TO
SEe IN POLITICS AROUND THE GLOBE; WHY THE EXTREMe POSI-
TIONS ON BOTH SIDES?

Here is where you are beginning to see the effects of the shift
we've been speaking of. This may seem surprising to you, as it
would appear that the shift in global consciousness would mean
a move toward unity, rather than division. However, in order to
experience unity, the divisions must be made clear. In order for
any healing to occur, whether it is within an individual, a collective, or a system, that which needs to be healed must be understood, and so in these early stages of the shift, you are seeing these
divisions being made clear in many ways. This may appear to be
quite disheartening; however, allow us to assure you that you are
only just beginning to see the uprising and groundswell of love
that is necessary for the real healing to begin.

Understand that the sense of division comes from fear. It is a
fear that the systems in which the population has placed all of its
trust and faith have failed them; it is a sense of needing to divide
in order to regroup into a more resonant type of system, or government, or culture. The old ways will not stand and the new ways
must have space made for them. As you witness in your own individual lives, any type of change requires a disintegration of the
old. And as the ego maintains a hold on that which is crumbling,
it creates suffering as the process unfolds.

Do not lose heart in the illusion of division that is occurring
before your eyes. Remember from whence you came; you began
as a single cell that only supported life when it began to divide,
and it was in that division of cells that the unity began, creating
the matter that houses you as a single organism, as a unit of consciousness, as a divine extension of Source—separate and individual and yet unified with the consciousness of all others and with
the supreme energy of Source.

Here, as your population stands within its energy, the true
division is only between love and fear. This is the basis of all division among living entities. For when one stands in love, there is

no division, and when one stands in fear, there is nothing but division. It is within each individual to choose, and there is no wrong choice, as fear is as necessary as love in creating change. Stay awake to your spiritual growth, and continue on with loving compassion for those who stand in fear. They are not to be pitied or conquered, but rather respected for their own views and what they are reflecting back to you about your own fears. As you begin to heal these fears within yourself, you will begin to see the healing in your culture.

IS THERe A HIGHLY EVOLVED CIVILIZATION NOW ACTIVE INSIDE EARTH? ACCORDING TO RAMTHA, CHANnELeD BY AUTHoR JZ KNIGHT, THE EARTH IS HOLIOW AND IS AT LEAST PARTIALIY POPULATED.

Let us just say that there are infinite universes within universes, and dimensional spaces within dimensions, and material worlds within worlds. Our existence is not limited by the material that you know, and countless dimensional spaces exist all around you. Your life experience is multidimensional and unlimited; to place these dimensional spaces in a particular material space and time is not exactly the truth, although it does help our limited understanding to grasp the concept of a multidimensional reality. This is quite a roundabout way of saying that in the physical sense of your current dimensional reality, another race of beings living within your Earth is not the truth. But as a form of multidimensional reality that is quite removed from your understanding of the material existence of life, there is.

WHO IS RESPONSIBLE FoR CROP CIRCLES?

There's been quite a bit of controversy concerning the originator of these types of crop formations in various parts of the world. We have been observing these phenomena on your planet for a while now, and it is our premise that while there are some formations that are made by the hand of man, there are others

79

that are unmistakably real and created by something above your planet's surface.

These signatures from above often convey messages to those who have the patience and knowledge to hear them.

For instance, we believe the crop circle that appeared in Wiltshire, U.K., in August 2015, which incorporates many versions of the number nine within it, was created to assure mankind that it is nearing the final part of this current stage of universal energy, and that its passing will usher in a new, gentler energy. There have been many who have been feeling the effects of the recent shift, and this has not always been a pleasant feeling, but we believe this indicates the passing of this feeling and a movement toward a more integrated way of being. The number nine contains all the other numbers within it, and it signifies completion and rest, which may be what is being urged here.

There are some specific dates alluded to on this formation, and they indicate those times when the solar, planetary, and atmospheric conditions are quite in alignment with what is necessary for the highest degree of energetic support for this shift; there are numeric calculations that create the type of symmetry that is seen in what you term sacred geometry, and the frequency of these energetic shapes allows for the flow of certain types of energy. The beings who create some of these formations are well versed in the interplay of these energies and wish to help you discover the beauty of them through the beauty of their work and the symmetry involved in making them. The air of mystery and the depth of meaning in these shapes is quite a remarkable gift and we would urge you to perceive these formations in that way and find meaning in that mystery. There are powerful forces at play in your atmosphere in this moment in time; stay centered in the beauty of that energy and don't fear any unusual shifts you may perceive, as they are all in your highest good.

WHO ARE THE SPIRITUALLY AWARE MASTERS OF THE HUMAN WORLD TODAY?

While there are many in the field who have achieved fame through their work, it is important to note that the most powerful leaders and teachers are not always those who are in the public eye. There are, placed among the small towns and communities, beings who simply live their lives in an unconventional way. They are not always the spiritual teachers; they are the artists, the free thinkers, the anarchists, the unconventional who stand out in their determination to be the highest expression of themselves in this lifetime. Their presence in the world is often the greatest form of influence on the masses, who tend toward a more conventional and less self-expressive form of life. Of course, those spiritual leaders who do achieve a certain amount of fame may be very important as well, and there are up-and-coming masters who will challenge previous notions of spirituality and religion, yourself among them. You must understand there is great wisdom scattered throughout your world, and its origin is the Source energy that hums with an increasing frequency within the spirits of those who are being called forward. You will recognize them as brothers and sisters.

HAVE YOU EVER COMMUNICATED WITH SOME OF EARTH'S BEST-KNOWN SPIRITUAL MASTERS, LIKE BUDDHA, KRISHNA, MUHAMMAD, OR OTHERS? SINCE JESUS IS BEST KNOWN TO ME AND TO MOST OF MY READERS, ANY THOUGHTS FROM HIM?

Yes, we have connected with the energy of these and other spiritual masters; in fact, you may be interested to know that these masters are not exclusive to Earth. They have equivalent aspects of their beings existent in other worlds, such as ours.

This does not mean that we depict them as human, or that their followers believe in the same religious dogma as appears on your planet; it means that as with all forms of consciousness, these higher beings are multidimensional and can send aspects of themselves that carry their wisdom and teaching to the far reaches of the universe and back, and that we can experience that wisdom in various physical and spiritual forms.

The teachings of these spiritual leaders come from the aspect of Source that provides the opportunity to connect with the highest level of one's being and to focus on love, connection, compassion, truthfulness, and accountability of one's actions as a means to form a stronger connection with the energy of Source, which is present within all. The appearance of these teachers at various times in history coincides with a wave of intention to find that higher connection in order to cope with and respond to severe challenges in one's social environment. At the time of Jesus's appearance on Earth, there were many challenges in corrupt leadership, which was causing great suffering among the masses, and so the global cry for help was met with the physical incarnation of a high-vibrational spiritual master.

It is important to point out, however, that the physical incarnation of these masters was not meant to create objects of worship, fear, or a sort of spiritual hierarchy that places the human (or any other physical being) at the bottom of the list. These spiritual masters incarnated into your world in such a way that they would be seen as regular humans, no different from any laborer or peasant, so that those around them could understand the divinity that lives in their own souls. The teaching of all these masters centered upon helping others recognize the power, wisdom, and love that lies at the heart of each and every conscious being, and the intention was that in understanding and honoring one's own divinity, a greater balance could be achieved in the treatment and support of the masses.

As with any teaching, however, the lesson can only be integrated at the level of the individual's belief system and choice of truth. As such, those who understood that Jesus's teachings were meant to be about empowerment and self-love saw the threat to their own delusional power, and so they executed him. And when it was clear that this act only created a stronger force behind the lessons, they created religious dogma that skewed the teaching and made it seem to be advocating fear, judgment, and threats to the soul if one's behavior did not meet certain standards. Please know that the original words and teaching of all spiritual masters never included any such concepts; it is a manipulation of their words by those who seek to use them to control the masses, which has created religious dogma advocating fear.

At the heart of every religion, just as at the heart of everything, from the smallest atomic speck of energy to the whole of the universe, lies the energy of love. And anything that induces fear is not centered in this love, so it is not the truth. This is at the heart of all the teachings of all the spiritual masters you have experienced in your world, and those we have knowledge of in ours. These masters come forth as the living embodiment of Source, as conduits of the love and power of Source, with the intention of helping those who choose to listen to become aware of the truth that EVERYONE is this living embodiment and conduit of the divine. They did not incarnate with the intention to be worshipped or praised or feared. They came with the intention to reveal the truth. As such, ALL who seek to reveal the truth of each individual's divinity are divine masters in their own right.

Accepting the role of divine teacher and master and choosing an incarnation in which these teachings are central to their life's purpose is evidence of these teachers' ascension and evolution to a supremely high energetic frequency. Only those who are willing to face the inherent persecution and judgment by the masses who fear the truth and who feel threatened by a population that cannot be controlled by the force of untruths will choose this path. And so, these master teachers continue their work within the spiritual realms of divinity. However, there are many among the ranks of ordinary incarnated beings, both human and nonhuman, who have chosen similar roles but in a much less public way, seeking to teach on a smaller scale, without much recognition or fame but with the same connection to the divine and the same intention to empower and inspire all they come into contact with toward their own highest level of being. These individuals may be recognized by a few but will never achieve the level of worship and praise that the divine masters faced. However, their work is just as holy, pure, and necessary.

As requested, we will bring forth some wisdom from the energy of Jesus:

In the current moment of time within your planet's history, in the current climate of fear and shifting energy, and within the intention to ascend beyond fear, hatred, and dogma, come legions of masters from the various realms, speaking through channelers, speaking through teachers and various leaders, speaking through the homeless and the billionaires, speaking through the persecuted and the worshipped, speaking words of love, compassion, and healing. My teachings are alive and well within the masses, in every sector of humanity on your planet, and the contrast to these teachings is the voice of fear. The fearful voice is becoming louder and more overwhelming for your people only for the purpose of inciting an uprising against it, only to allow the truth to emerge even more strongly, for through persecution and hatred comes an even stronger wave of love and understanding, which will stand up against anything that gives the illusion of power to that which is not in alignment with Source, for Source is the only power, the only energy that lies at the heart of all of creation. Do not seek the truth in churches, in the political arena, in the wealthy or famous. Instead, seek it within your own heart, for the energy of the heart is in direct alignment with the energy of Source, which is the supreme truth of all beings. YOU are the creator of your life, but not only your own life is created by the power of your being, but all of life, all of reality, all things in the universal system, and it is within that act of creation that you are truly expressing the will of the divine.

PART 3

THE GREATER UNIVERSE

These questions create the
opportunity to learn about broader
considerations beyond life on either
Brahoshka or Earth, and to learn
about universal truths presumably
applying to all forms of life that,
once known, will help us
flourish here and now.

CAN YOU EXPLAIN OUR RELATIONSHIP WITH DIVINE MIND (GOD)? AND CAN YOU EXPLAIN THE DISCONnECT WE often FEeL BETWEeN OURSELVES AND SOURCE?

The Divine Mind or Source energy is the basis of all energetic mass in the universe, and it is this energy that connects us to the essence of ourselves. Source energy is not just present when it is called upon, it is the current of force that energizes all matter and all energetic fields within the dimensional realms. Source is what animates us, and it is the originator of all aspects of being.

That being said, as energetic emanations of Source, we are inherently connected to this divine energy, and in fact, this energy runs through the very core of all living beings, tying us intrinsically to our origins in a mutually responsive connection that allows Source to experience the incarnated life through the energy of the individual, and allows the individual access to the limitless essence of Source.

As we are all aspects of this Divine Mind, we are also intrinsically connected to each other through this nonjudgmental and loving energy. This connection is also at the core of our beings, and it is in these moments of divine connection that we experience the greatest sense of wholeness and peace available to an incarnated being.

By the same token, we are each individual aspects of this Source energy, and as such, we express the different aspects through the individual nature of our personality and varying traits. We are provided with an ego, or a sense of separated selfhood, so that we are best able to exercise our individual free will and choice-making. It is within these acts of manifestation that we are exercising our divine powers of creation.

The sense of separation stems from this realization of our own individual nature, and from a belief structure that is built upon the idea of judgment, reward, and punishment. Instead of seeing ourselves as divine aspects of Source energy, these types of dogma create a sense of obligation to a separate and self-righteous leader who sits in judgment of His lowly offspring. Many are taught to experience themselves as children of a vengeful father who were created merely to please their creator with acts of worship and contrition. It is difficult to feel a sense of connection with an energy that stands ready to punish those who do not please it.

Many will lose their sense of divine connection because they feel unable to live up to the standards that are supposedly set by this higher power, and so they will eventually give up and find little pleasure in their lives, seeing themselves as inherently flawed beings who can never please their divine father. Still others will find joy in acts of service to their creator, but will never truly look within at the divinity that exists there. Instead, they will forever look outward to find that sense of connection and most likely will never feel what it is that they wish to feel.

Within each of these choices lies a divine experience that offers a different aspect of the evolution of the soul, and so it is important to remember that no choice is a wrong one for the experience of that being in this incarnation. Some may alternately choose such incarnations for the balance of experience known as karma and the richness of living many different types of incarnated lives to further educate and enlighten the soul.

And then there will be those who will heed the intuitive calling of the heart and soul that is acutely aware of this direct connection to Source energy and who will strive to honor that connection through the honoring of themselves, their lives, and their works. It is a fallacy to believe that Source requires an external sense of worship that involves a diminishing of the individual; rather, the true worship of Source is experienced through acts of self-love and self-care, expression of the gifts of the soul, and sharing of the inner light of the individual, as these are true expressions of the divine.

Source energy is ever flowing and ever moving through the energy of the incarnated being, and it is expressed through the inner senses, the intuition, and the creative expression of the individual. When one falls out of touch with these aspects of oneself—either as a result of social pressures or out of a sense of unreasonable expectations that one places on oneself—emotions become troubled and a sense of despair ensues. In this sense of despair lies loneliness and disconnection, not only with Source energy but with all other beings. The act of staying connected presents its own challenges, as the brain is wired with many volatile emotional responses to stimuli in the exterior world and is often ruled by the fears of the ego. It is through the spiritual practices of meditation, peaceful intention, and focus on the divine light within that one is most able to feel that ever-present connection and become aware of the subtle guidance presented by it. It is in those experiences of true connection that one is able to feel the authentic essence and nature of being; it is in the act of co-creation that one is truly expressing the divine light into a dimensional space of reality.

Therefore, it is Source that is at the essence of all creation, and as such, all creation is connected as vibrational frequency back to Source. All conscious beings are gifted with the sense of will—which is designed so that they can experience that sense of creation that is at the essence of Source—and we are able to decide what to do with that gift. As the origin and fundamental essence of all things, Source is ever present and continually involved in the act of manifestation through its own handiwork. We are not only connected to Source, we ARE Source in all of its infinite forms.

There is the question of divine intervention, or miracles affected by Source energy outside of the realm of individual expression of creation, and it is true that these do occur. As a function of creation, Source expresses itself through the synchronistic acts that can lead to physical healing, the bringing together of various soul beings, avoidance of disaster, and other miraculous events that cannot be explained by logical means. However, it is important to understand that although it appears as though these miracles are occurring outside of the normal human experience, they are directly connected to the will of the being experiencing them, and as such, they are also co-created by the individual in congruence with Source. We are created as partners, you see, and thus we bear the responsibility to simply use our will and our choices to create the reality we choose to experience. This includes the experiences that may be labeled as miraculous.

There are many truths to be found in religion surrounding the nature of God/Source/divine energy, and there are many contrived falsehoods. Some will cling to the falsehoods out of a sense of the comfort that is experienced when one feels that someone else is responsible for their experiences; there is an absolution of responsibility and an adoption of the role of victim to the whims of a loving but vengeful God. One only needs to follow certain rules in order to gain reward, and if one breaks those rules, one can find forgiveness through ritual. This is the construct of religion that was devised to exploit and assert control over the individual will.

At the heart of all religions, however, is the sense of a powerful, creative, and loving force that is ever present and alive in all things. The nature of this energy was once equated to the natural forces, and the energetic essence of God was said to be expressed in all natural aspects of being; the beauty of nature, the changing seasons, the mystery of the universe, all were seen as aspects of this divine presence. This, then, is the true expression of the divine: in the energetic structure of all things, in the spiritual essence of your own being, and in the divine will that is present within you.

YOU ARE A COLLECTIVE OF EIGHT. ARE YOU AS ABLE TO CONNECT WITH US AND EXPLORE THE UNIVERSE INDIVIDUALLY, OR DO YOU NEED THE COLLECTIVE ENERGY OF YOUR GROUP?

As a rule, we travel in groups. This is due to many factors. The energy of the collective is far greater than that of one individual, and so we find that our ability to communicate is better and that the energy we spend on the work we do is more evenly distributed. There is much to be said for combining forces toward a common goal, and so we have made it a standard practice to do this work collectively.

We also find that there is a sense of safety when traveling and working as a group; for instance, when one of us has an issue with the energetic transference, another is always available to assist, guide, and reassure. The confidence that comes from this knowledge alleviates the fear of traveling alone; therefore, the experience is much more positive than it might otherwise be.

In addition, we find that as a group we are able to share thoughts, ideas, and suggestions about how best to accomplish what we have set out to do. For example, when we are answering your questions, we will consult among ourselves for the best possible way to respond, and we find that those joint responses are much richer, wiser, and more comprehensive than any one being could offer.

While it is absolutely possible for just one of us to project the energy of consciousness through universal time and space, it is not something we would recommend or practice, as we have found that the benefits of the collective eliminate the desire we may have once had for traveling alone.

Do you work with other planetary civilizations?

We have worked with other civilizations in varying ways. Not all of our work is as intensely focused; sometimes it is simply to educate them about the vastness of universal energy and to help them place themselves in the grand scheme of the universe and its design. Planting that seed of thought was often enough to create an acceleration of consciousness from which they could experience the richness of their life experience with the intended intensity and use it to its greatest advantage. We will disengage our energy when our intended purpose has been served, or when it is clear that our attempts are being met with too much resistance to be useful.

Did life once exist on Mars or elsewhere in our solar system? If so, are we descendants of such life, as claimed by many theorists? Is our past so straightforward as to always have yes or no answers? Or are there different pasts, as there are different futures?

The truth, as you are intuiting here, is not quite so simple and straightforward as some may believe. Even the truth that we are suggesting to you has its flaws in the reality of our multidimensional existence. In this sense of reality, there are no absolutes, and so while there may not be scientific evidence of the evolution of life throughout the universe, it certainly exists, and the theory of multiple pasts that you are referring to here has a certain amount of truth to it.

Understand that life has always and will always exist in some form. These life-forms may not be what you would now consider to be legitimate expressions of life, and their forms may be so far out of the realm of your understanding of what life is that you would not even comprehend them as an aspect of creation. This limited understanding is by design, as it creates a narrow comprehension of reality, which is necessary for you to focus on the here and now of the life you are currently living. However, we would like to suggest that you consider that there is an infinite number of ways that the universe can be expressed as a form of consciousness, and that Source is present in all of those expressions. As such, there do exist such unexpected life-forms, and they are valid and real.

And so we would like to suggest to you that ALL the planets have, at one time, in some dimensional space, and in some field of conscious existence, had life of some form on them. And that ALL of these forms of life—whether they are in your current dimensional expression of time and space or some other—are connected energetically. This is why the sense that you are not alone as a species or that there are others present in the universe feels resonant with so many; you intrinsically know that you are connected to much more than what is present in your current field of awareness.

And so, we would agree with some of the theories to which you refer, but we would also say that they are not the complete truth, and that there are many other theories that contain bits and pieces of truth, as that truth is limited by the deliberately narrow field of belief that is possible in the human brain.

This, we understand, is quite the esoteric answer, and not quite as concrete as you may have been hoping for, but we would suggest that you sit within the immense possibility of it and see how it feels, rather than limit it to what you can intellectually understand.

CAN YOU EXPLAIN THE ANGELIC REALM? HOW MUCH CAN THEY HELP US? IF THEY HELP US, DOES THEIR INTERVENING DENY US THE OPPORTUNITY TO LEARN OF OUR OWN POWER?

The angelic realm consists of higher vibrational beings who have not incarnated into the physical and who have agreed to remain in the nonphysical state with the purpose of aiding physical beings on their life paths. Understand that there is a certain amount of preplanning that occurs when the soul being agrees to incarnate into the physical. It is sometimes the case that the soul being, in its state of freedom from the heavy constraints of a physical life, becomes overzealous in its blueprinting of its life structure.

Once they have entered the physical realm, these beings may find that some of the obstacles and challenges inherent in their path become a bit too much for them to handle. There may be moments of despair and grief, sadness and frustration, loneliness and emptiness, which can become overwhelming for those who are not able to see the higher purpose of their existence. It is in these moments that these higher beings may be called into assistance.

The high vibration of these beings can influence those in the physical realm in a number of ways: It can lend comfort in moments of despair; it can cause slight alterations in the physical path, which may alleviate some suffering; it can accelerate the raising of consciousness and assist those on a spiritual path in understanding their own divinity.

In this way, these beings are seen as partners or mentors to those they assist, and their actions are not seen as interference with the choices of physical beings. Again, this assistance is agreed upon in advance, and so an angelic being will not intervene without some type of request, either from the consciousness of the being or from the calling of the soul.

As with all energetic beings, the angelic realm is an extension of Source energy, and as such, it is in service to all beings with love and compassionate guidance. The physical being is free to experience free will in the response to this intervention; it can be seen as a gift from Source and confirmation of the higher realms, or it can be seen as simple coincidence or luck. Whatever choice is made will once again have an effect on the trajectory of that being's particular life path, and no choice is a wrong one.

There are many angelic beings available to you at any given moment, and within those beings are infinite aspects of themselves, which means they are available in an unlimited way. The calling in of an angel does not diminish their ability to assist others, and that call will always be heeded and answered, even when you feel it is being ignored. There are those whose responses are quiet and subtle, and those whose energy is felt by the physical being as a palpable, physically manifested shift in their material environment. These aspects of being are deliberate, and will be in resonance with the life path of the individual.

There are many levels of nonphysical beings that serve different purposes and fulfill different roles. The angelic realm encompasses a vast array of beings whose work is all equally important, but there are those with the highest frequency and closest aspect to Source whose energy and awareness can be felt by those with certain sensitivities. These beings are what you refer to as the archangels, and while many of the ideas about these beings in your teachings are correct, there are also some misconceptions about them that are simply human constructs and have no basis in the truth. For instance, in your artwork and visual depictions of angels, they are most often shown with wings. This depiction occurred because the human was not able to understand how a being could move through time and space in an unlimited way without some physical assistance to transport them. The magical element of flying created an otherworldly aspect of these beings and explained how they could cover great distances unhindered by the limited physical body. In actuality, these beings do not require wings as they are nonphysical beings who are not limited by time and space. However, if they choose to create a visual image of themselves to those they are serving, they may choose to present themselves in this traditional way so that the nature of their being is made clear to the person who is observing them.

The intervention of the angelic realm will always be done with the highest intention to assist the physical being with some aspect of their path, which has become out of control or overwhelming, and so it is within those moments of assistance that the physical being is able to be enriched on their path, rather than having their own power of manifestation taken away. The angelic realm answers calls for assistance, and so their assistance will come only as a last resort, when all else has failed and it is clear that some help is required. It is important for you to understand that none of you is traveling this physical path alone, no matter what is reflected to you by your outside world. There are always angelic beings, guides, loved ones in spirit, and other beings whose purpose is to assist and uplift you as you travel the sometimes challenging road of your life.

CAN YOU EXPLAIN HOW NUMEROLOGY WORKS, IF IT DOES IN FACT WORK?

We would like to begin by pointing out that all life consists of the structure of patterns. From the atomic level to the cellular level, there are patterns that create a grid of energy needed to support a system. Consider the natural world around you and how it consists of a series of patterns, grids, and structural repetitions that support mass, weight, and depth. This is true of all energy and matter in the universe; even energy that appears to be chaotic supports some type of pattern within it. The minds of mathematicians, artists, musicians, physicists, and accountants alike are well aware of how patterns create systems, and systems create order.

The numerical patterns that are tapped into when studying the field of numerology capitalize on these patterns and structures, and within those patterns are found repeating energetic forces that influence the energetic structure of the energy of the human being, thereby affecting personality, emotions, and tendencies. As such, all aspects of your identity contain within them certain patterns that can be used to reflect aspects of your character. And since all aspects of your being are integrated into your identity—your birth date, name, astrological arrangement, birthplace, ancestry, genetic composition, and more—each aspect can be examined to uncover certain patterns that affect your personality. Numerology is just one of these types of patterns, and it can be quite the revealing study.

WHAT ABOUT TAROT CARDS? HOW CAN THEY BE READ WHEN THEY SEeM PURELY RANDOM?

There are many tools that can be utilized to assist in the focus needed to tap into the higher senses of intuition and so-called psychic abilities. As sentient beings in an existence that is full of distractions and material concerns, the higher senses are often negated in favor of the intellect and logic. These tools create a point of focus that is needed to tune out the distractions of the material world and bring the energy into the higher senses, which is where the connection to truth and Source energy is accessible.

The system of the tarot allows an activation of the intuitive senses both in the drawing of seemingly random cards and the interpretation of the same. As there is intention in the action of drawing and reading the cards, there is nothing about that action that is truly random, as intention is the driving force behind all actions and their results. Tapping into the higher intuitive energy allows access to higher wisdom and knowledge, and as representatives of certain aspects of the life path, the tarot cards can help place focus on those areas that need attention in the life of the card reader's subject.

As with the patterns of numerology, astrology, genealogy, and other influential aspects of energetic existence, the tarot allows for deeper understanding and wisdom to emerge that is not accessible through the confines of intellectual thought. And as with all excavations into the richness of the incarnated experience, it is the intention that is the driving force, no matter what method or tool is used.

DO SOULS HAVE DIFFERENT AGES? ARE THERE INCARNATIONAL ARCHETYPES, SUCH AS THOSE TAUGHT BY AUTHOR CHELSEA QUINN YARBRO: SERVER, PRIEST, ARTISAN, SAGE, WARRIOR, KING, AND SCHOLAR? IF POSSIBLE, CAN YOU SPEAK TO THE RELEVANCE OF BOTH SOUL AGES AND ARCHETYPES?

The idea of a soul age is based on the premise that there is a linear progression from infancy to maturity in the soul, as there is in the physical lifetime of an individual. While it is true that the soul is enhanced and evolves through the experiences in the physical realm, and therefore will experience a certain type of maturation as it accumulates these experiences, there is not exactly an infancy stage of the soul as is described in this work. The soul is formed as an extension of Source energy, and as such, it is whole and complete at its inception. There is some truth, however, in the notion that souls who have not experienced many incarnations in the physical realm will have different challenges than those who have experienced many physical lifetimes. The process is not quite as pronounced as it is in the lifetime of a physical entity, which begins with a sense of helplessness and dependency at its inception, passes through a maturation process through learning and exploration, and ends in a state of mental and spiritual maturity. The soul does not only experience its growth and evolution in the physical; there is much to be learned and experienced in the nonphysical, and so an aspect of the soul that chooses to incarnate in the physical is not quite as immature and devoid of experience as this notion may suggest.

The truth in this theory surrounds the idea that those with limited physical experience will tend to choose experiences that are rooted in the physical; they may have more issues with the physical body, material possessions, and security. This is because their initial experiences will be all about living life in the physical realm, and so this foundational experience will be what sets the tone for any subsequent incarnations that this soul aspect may choose. This does not mean, however, that these "newer" souls will choose the most challenging aspects of a physical existence; in fact, they will most likely choose fewer and less severe challenges as they discover how much they are able to withstand. It is the most evolved and experienced soul who chooses the most severe challenges in the physical life, such as chronic illness; physical, mental, and psychological challenges; and severe struggles with poverty, abuse, or other types of suffering. Only those who feel they are ready to take on these types of challenges will incarnate with this kind of life framework.

Again, this does not mean that the aspect of the soul that chooses an experience in the physical is in any way flawed or lacking; it means that the soul being chooses these experiences to enhance its potential and enrich its broad spectrum of experience. No soul being is created as lacking; it is whole and complete at its inception, but with plenty of room to grow and learn in every possible way.

More evolved souls may also choose a life of spiritual inquiry and exploration, as their exploration of life through the physical experiences has already enriched them, and they are aware that it's time to explore the higher realms from the perspective of the physical form.

Be aware that in the nonphysical state of being, learning occurs at an accelerated pace, and the experience is not limited by time and space. Applying the linear constraints of time to the evolution of the soul is placing limits on an unlimited experience for the sake of creating understanding, and so, while there is truth in various forms in this work, these truths are being explained and translated through the linear construct of the brain of the human who is channeling them. (This, by the way, also occurs in the work we are doing with this channel; since we are aware of it, we are usually able to compensate for it.)

The archetypes of experience are symbolic references to the types of life journeys chosen by the aspect of the soul as it maps out its physical path. These seven archetypes contain within them many different life experiences, and so there is much truth to the notion that the symbolic aspects of these roles will be the guiding factor in the manifestation of the foundational life structure. To limit these to seven, however, is not quite accurate. So once again, while there is truth to the idea of archetypes, or symbols of the physical life experience, these symbols are not fully represented here.

It can also be said that every incarnation will have aspects of all of these archetypes to some degree, but that some may be more dominant than others. As the soul evolves and makes choices about its life path on its journeys in the physical, these archetypes may change; it is built into the structure of the life path that the individual can alter its course and choose other types of experience as it goes along. And so, the aspect of the soul that chooses to incarnate may decide originally on the experience of a server, but at some point in that role may decide to evolve out of it and into one of the other roles for the betterment of the experience. This is the aspect of divine will, which is taken into account at the time of designing the physical experience; as such, the soul aspect does not place too much expectation on the path its incarnated expression may choose.

As with most human theories about the spiritual world and the soul's journey, there are limitations, misinterpretations, and oversimplified categorizations that simply do not exist outside of the confines of the human brain. So we would like to suggest that you view our answers as a foundational structure of truth that can be expanded upon and explored more and more deeply to find the ultimate truth. But also understand that some aspects of non-physical existence are simply not comprehensible by the physical matter of the brain.

HOW ARE YOU ABLE TO BE IN MORE THAN ONE PLACE AT ONE TIME? PLEASE DESCRIBE HOW YOU EXPERIENCE YOUR MULTIDIMENSIONAL NATURE. FOR EXAMPLE, MY AWARENESS IS SHARPLY

FOCUSED ON A SINGLE HERe AND NOW. I HAVE SUBTLE MEMO-
RIES AND INTUITION I CAN TAP INTO SIMULTANEOUSLY TO BEING
PHYSICALlY PRESeNT IN MY HERe AND NOW. You, HOWEVeR,
ARE ABLE TO LEND YOUR AWaRENEss TO TRACY AND ACTIVELY
FoRM INTENT, RECeIVE MY QUESTIONS, RELAY ANSWERS, ETC.,
ALl WHILE LIVING YOUR PHYSICAL LIVES AND, PRESUMABLY,
FUNCTIONING WITH AN AWaRENEss THAT EXPANDS ELSEWHERe.
HoW DO YOU PERCEIVE ALl OF THIS? IT SEeMS LIKE YOU ARE
ABLE TO BE IN SEVeRAL PLACES AT THE SAME TIME. CoR-
RECT? HOW DO YOU KNOW WHERe AND WHEN TO FOCUS YOUR
ATtENTION?

As a being who is experiencing your life as a three-dimensional concept, you are only able to consciously perceive those things that are held within those three dimensions. So you can perceive length, depth, and height, and that is the limit of your experience of reality. The introduction of another dimension to this reality, therefore, would not necessarily be perceived by you, as your brain would not know how to process it and so it would be filtered out of your brain's perception as an anomaly or mistake in perception. This, then, demonstrates that the brain is limited in its perception not only by what it believes to be true, but by the very nature of its structure, which is programmed to perceive only that which it can make sense of and that which it is in the habit of experiencing.

The truth, however, is that right now there are other aspects of your being that are experiencing reality in other types of dimensional space, in other constructions of time, and in other parts of the universe. Your perception of reality is limited, however, by the singular focus of this perceived space and time, and so it is not possible for your brain to comprehend the realities outside of the one it occupies. It is even difficult for you to imagine this, as the brain will resist it as fantasy or imagination, yet the soul will resonate with this truth if you will allow yourself to feel it.

In our experience, the aspect of ourselves that is going about our lives on our home planet is mostly oblivious to the aspect that is traveling. It is focused on the here and now that it is perceiving through its own form of brain and its own perception of reality. The only difference is that we are fully aware that we are doing this work, and we will have times when we will integrate the knowledge of these experiences into the consciousness living on our home planet so that these experiences can be recorded and reported back to those in the physical who are gathering the data. Other than those times, the physical aspects of our beings are not aware of the nonphysical aspects that are experiencing things outside of the physical reality.

This does not mean that we have split ourselves into multiple beings. We are still, each of us, one being, separate individuals, and one incarnation that is, in its state of being multidimensional, able to be bi-locational—that is, to exist in multiple locations, dimensions, and spaces at the same time. Your quantum physicists have proven this to be a reality in the laboratory; however, they have not yet realized the full implication of this discovery as it pertains to the human being, and how the energetic aspects of an individual could also be multidimensional and bi-locational.

The best way to demonstrate this to you is to point out how you dream every night. These dreams serve various purposes: some are functions of the brain, a sort of memory dump or data release that allows information to be filtered through and released. Others are evidence of multidimensional or astral travel, in which an aspect of your being travels through various dimensional spaces. If these experiences are translated into the memory portion of your brain, the images will mostly be interpreted as some fantasy or nonsensical series of events. Your brain will simply believe that it is just another dream, because it cannot understand the true nature of the energetic, multidimensional being. So the consciousness that you experience in this lifetime is focused solely on what it is experiencing from one moment to the next in one single, three-dimensional space, in one single moment of time, and in one single aspect of reality that it believes to be its only truth.

In reality, there are many truths and many levels of being within your one soul, and these levels of being are experiencing their own focused reality, oblivious to all the others, believing that their own singularity is all that exists.

Rarely, there will be crossovers into these other dimensional spaces, usually stimulated by a state of altered consciousness brought on by chemical stimulants, illness, or focused spiritual travel. However, the experience is not likely to be well understood by the brain, and so it will become distorted and mystical, and may seem like it was either concocted in the imagination or a type of hallucination.

What we do is not much different from what you do in every second of your existence. We have simply found a way to consciously and deliberately manipulate this multidimensional travel through the power of will and the understanding of the workings of energy.

ARE YOU AND I IN TOUCH AT OTHER LEVeLS OF AWaRENeSs? SURELY IF I AM SO KEeNLY INTEReSTED IN YOU AND ALl YOU HAVE TO SHARE, MY GREATER SELF (oR SELVES) oR MY OTHER-DIMENSIONAL SELVES ARE TOo. CAN I WILl THEM TO fiND YOU? CAN YOU WILl YOURSELVES TO fiND THOSE OTHER ASPECTS OF ME?

We can only assure you that they have and will continue to find us, in many of our own multidimensional forms. In the illusions of space and time, we have most assuredly met before and will meet again, as it is in the will of our soul beings that we do so. This will transcends the will of the physical being, and while your own will has an influence on your multidimensional incarnations, it is the will of the soul that determines the paths of these many existences. Any more than that, we are not privileged to know. And it is in that unknowing that the true wonder of existence lies.

THERE HAVE BEEN MANY REFERENCES BY VARIOUS SPIRITUAL TEACHERS, AND YOURSELVES, ABOUT THE COSMIC SHIFTS OF ENERGY THAT ARE OCCURRING ON EARTH. CAN YOU ADDRESS THIS?

Yes. Specifically, we'd like to discuss the need for those who are feeling some of the emotional effects of the recent cosmic shifts in energy to take some time for themselves through the process and not to overdo the work that they perform, either at home or on the job. We are discovering a certain amount of physical fatigue comes with the energetic shifts that have been encountered, and so it is important that the body takes advantage of any time it may have available for rest, relaxation, and calm. There are many energies at play in the current moment, and these energies can cause some chaos in the energy field of sensitive people, causing insomnia, irritability, impatience, and a sense of withdrawal.

If you are finding any of these symptoms plaguing you, please be assured that such shifts subside when the planetary aspects and your moon return to a less energetic alignment and some other cosmic forces quiet down. Understand that there are strong magnetic and solar forces at play in these early to middle years of your 21st century, which can create an energetic storm of quite some magnitude. You may find yourself experiencing some challenges through these shifts, but it is important to realize that these challenges will create a sense of the warrior in you that will be needed as you go forth through these pockets of energy. Be assured that these shifts are all leading to the highest form of energetic vibration, which is necessary for the advancement and evolution of your planet and all of its beings. It is quite a privilege to be alive during this time of accelerated growth and higher awareness.

Do not despair in any of the current challenges in your political and leadership arenas, as these are only serving to bring the need for global change to light among those who have resisted these changes. None of these challenges is a lost cause, and we would like you to see that your world is waking up and standing firm in its resolve to create better systems that serve all people and protect all living things with the compassion of the soul and the wisdom of the heart. This is the law of the universe and it is developing just as it should. Take heart in the progress that you see and do not let the ignorance of the few discourage you in your path toward the shift. All who hear us are part of this shift and we encourage you to focus on those things that are coming into the light of day, which will allow them to be transfigured into a more positive state of being for all.

We are quite amazed at the way your people are responding to these challenges and we send you great love and the energy of our thoughts, which foresee a new world blossoming under your feet.

HOW DOES A "GREATER REALITY" EXIST WITHOUT TIME AND SPACE?

In any explanation that goes beyond the constructs of space and time, it is important to understand that all physical matter is inherently limited. This is by design, as it is within these limitations that one is able to experience one's true potential to extend beyond, above, and outside those physical limitations into the realm of unlimited energy. The physical matter of the brain, which processes all received information, has limitations built into it that will not allow it to make sense of anything other than its perceived experience of time and space. This linear construct creates the illusion of progress that is necessary for the will to achieve its aims. Without it, the will would not be motivated by change and growth, and as such, would not experience the magical elements of choice-making and learning. These limitations exist only while in the physical, however, and so it is with this very clear intention that one decides to experience the incarnated physical existence.

When one is in a nonphysical state, the reality of a time-space construct evaporates, and one is left with the totality of experience as a whole, complete being. This does not mean that the experience of linear time is not possible; one can choose to return to a somewhat altered sense of time so that the context of experience can be more clearly measured; however, it is not always necessary for one who experiences existence in the nonphysical to delineate that experience within the framework of time, as the physical limitations of brain function no longer exist and so understand-ing is greatly expanded into realms that are beyond your present mode of comprehension.

Suffice to say that the nonphysical aspect of being, or what you consider the soul being, exists within a conglomeration of all experience—past, present, and future—and all dimensional aspects of being, and it is within those experiences that the evo-lution of the soul being occurs. As a directly connected aspect of Source, it is within those experiences that Source is able to con-nect with all aspects of being without the limitations of physical matter. Every aspect of your experience, every moment of your existence, every microcosm of your being is divinely connected to Source beyond the limitations of the processing of informa-tion through the physical matter of your brain, beyond the phys-ical limitations of life and death, beyond the gravitational pull of your planet and the physical universe, beyond the emotional and instinctual aspects of your physical existence. But every one of those experiences enhances and enriches ALL of existence through the aspect of Source. This is what is meant by the concept of oneness.

So while it is nearly impossible for you to consider an existence that does not base its evolution on the linear constructs of time and space, we would like you to consider those brief moments you have already experienced that seemed quite timeless; those moments of being that were so focused on the present moment that time seemed to disappear and all that was left was that singu-lar moment that contained all of your existence. These moments are brief and fleeting within the physical realm, but it is within these moments that one can catch a glimpse of the reality of non-physical existence.

Therefore, it is quite a noble pursuit to practice this expan-sion of energetic existence, which goes beyond the limitations of understanding, as it is within those moments of allowing and acceptance without clear understanding that the true mystical experience of beingness can occur. You are an unlimited being, experiencing a limited aspect of your existence through physi-cal matter and the constraints of time and space so that you can experience the great joy of expanding beyond those limitations and truly and completely feeling those unlimited aspects of your being through the process of manifestation, through the overcoming of hardships, through the expansion of your mind into the realms of the unknown. We would like to encourage you to see these experiences as among some of the greatest gifts that may stem from your choice to be alive as you now are, as there is no other way of experiencing them than through this choice.

HOW CAN THERe BE GROWTH AND EXPANSION, oR IGNoRANCE LEADING TO KNOWLEDGE, IF THERe ARE NOT DEfiNITIONS OF BEFoRE AND AftER? HOW CAN AN ENTITY EVeN PROCESs oR CONTEMPLATE A SENTENCE WITHOUT TIME? THERe MUST BE SOME OTHER MEASUREMeNT oR FOUNDATION THAT HOLDS CONTEXT AND REFeRENCE POINTS TOGETHER?

Here, in your current realm of existence, there are certain expectations (learned through experience and culture) about the nature of reality that create an irrefutable construct of beginnings and endings, progression and expansion. Any other type of experience outside of that expectation is nearly impossible for your brain to comprehend or even begin to imagine. And yet, the experience of time that you are used to is only one of many types of time perception within a multidimensional universe.

It is true that most beings in the universe have some sense of progressive time, and this would include those things you would construe as beginnings and endings, starts and stops, and evolutionary progression. However, in some realms time is more malleable and the beings within that structure have the opportunity to slip backward and forward in time, with the present moment being a sort of home base for the incarnated experience. There is still a linear concept of time, but it is not quite so rigid as your experience on Earth. This sort of time slippage creates a unique experience of time and the progression of an individual's life path in these realms is not always based on a linear progression but on the weight and clarity of experiences in the present and in other periods of time.

The concept of no time in the spiritual realm is not quite what it appears to be, as there is still a progression of experience and the opportunity to learn, move forward in time, and grow; however, the signposts or delineation of the passage of time is not part of that experience, so the progression of time is not experienced in the same way as it is in the physical. As mentioned earlier, you have likely experienced incidents where time seemed to stop, or when you lost all perception of the passage of time and it appeared to speed up. You may have even experienced a time anomaly where you seem to have lost or gained time while you were focused on something else. This is because you were in a moment of detachment from the deeply ingrained expectations of how time operates, and so you were experiencing how it feels to be in a realm of no time. There was still a linear progression, but the concept of seconds, minutes, and hours slipped from your focus and you experienced a sort of suspended animation.

Another concept of time is one in which all time is happening at once. This is quite difficult to imagine, even impossible, as it places us in a state of no space to occupy and no clear form of existence if that existence in time cannot be somehow measured. Again, this concept does not eliminate the here and now or the progression from one thing to another; instead, it means that all aspects of existence in all moments of time can be accessed and visited. The past, present, and future can be experienced in any moment, as they all exist within the same framework. There is no reality that is completely gone, nor any that has not yet occurred. All realities exist, and as such, can be met within the experience of the here and now.

The struggles with these concepts come from the belief in a singularity as being the sole experience of existence. The belief that you, as a living being, are ONE being in space and time; that time is experienced as ONE moment to the next moment; that there is ONE consciousness experiencing these moments; and that we are completely self-contained individuals within ONE universe. These beliefs eliminate any understanding of the true nature of all existence and all time, which is that there are an infinite number of ways to experience existence, time, space, and beingness. This is demonstrated even among your fairly small human population; there are humans existing among you now with much different concepts of time and space, and a much different sense of awareness about themselves and their place among their fellow beings and the universe. There are those whom you would label as mentally disabled, or cognitively challenged, whose brain function and sense of consciousness creates such a different sense of reality that you pity them for not having a "normal" life, when in reality, their experience is actually more aligned with the experience of spiritual existence.

The common factor in all experiences of time and space among conscious beings is the ability to make choices, whether those choices are limited to what is being thought and believed, what physical movements and actions are being taken, where to focus one's energetic attention, or how to perceive and make sense of one's experience; the awareness of time and space is largely dictated by choice. And within those choices lies the ability to evolve, change, and transmute one's being into other forms of existence without judgment, without a sense of evolution being the only reason for existence, and without a sense of hierarchy or ascension. Ascension can still occur, but it is not the sole purpose of existence; one is not judged by their progress toward a certain state of energetic frequency. The supreme joy of being lies simply within that state of existence in no-time, no-space, and fully connected to the pure, loving energy of Source.

SAFE TO SAY, YOU HAVE NO IDEA OF CREATION'S ORIGINS?

The concept of infinity is a difficult one to grasp, even for those of a higher consciousness and understanding of Source energy. This is a deliberate construct in our state of consciousness, as it gives us a solid framework with which to build our life experience. But we are connected with the knowledge of an infinite universe, with no beginning and no end. This is in alignment with our cyclical experience of time, the notion that the beginning and end are one and the same, that our existence as energetic beings is timeless and formless among the vast beauty and wisdom of infinite love. And so, while there is a certain comfort in the notion of beginnings and endings, and we, as beings who are still connected to a physical existence, have difficulty truly understanding the notion of no time, no limits, and no real point of origin, we have an acceptance of this as truth, and it is quite a beautiful truth at that.

PART 4

BUILDING
A BETTER
WORLD

Given their hindsight and present worldviews (both worlds), I wondered how Frank would look forward to the infinite possibilities that exist for us— and for them. More specifically, how can we, on Earth, better understand and harness all that Frank's answers imply concerning universal energies and our innate (if unknown) abilities, with an emphasis on our individual and collective spiritual development?

PLEASE TELL US ABOUT THE POWERS AND PURPOSE OF IMAGINATION.

There is a great deal to be said for the process of imagining and visualizing in advance of actually performing or creating that which is desired. The imagination is a rich and fertile ground for creating that which you wish to see in your sense of material reality, and it is the breeding ground for all conscious acts of creation.

The word *imagination* is a vague and ephemeral term referring not to a specific part of the brain or a material element of the body, but to a certain type of sense; it is a sense of anticipation and expectation made real in the mind and psyche of the individual. This sense of that which has not yet materialized in the physical world can be a positive, high-vibrational scenario or it can be a scenario that causes a low-vibrational effect that you term *worry*. It is worry that causes a great deal of stress and anxiety, and it is important to note that worry is simply the act of imagining something going wrong.

With any use of the imagination, there is a mental, emotional, and physical reaction to that which is being imagined; it is very similar, if not identical, to the reaction that would occur if the things being imagined took place in the physical world, and it is this reaction, or response to the mental stimuli, that can cause feelings of excitement, dread, fear, or joy. These reactions are dictated solely by the mental images that one conjures up, but the energy surrounding the responses has a far-reaching effect, causing an energetic response that triggers a sense of expectation in the energy field and an attraction of like energy. And so, while the scenario being created in the energetic field of imagination may not precipitate exactly the same scenario in the material world, the energy of what is attracted will be very similar and will match the frequency of the vibration of the imagination.

It is exactly the same process as if you were creating some material thing with your hands and eyes; you first imagine what it is that you wish to create. This may take the form of a sketch or drawing, a blueprint, a description, or a computer-generated image that is the first level of the manifestation of that which has been imagined. From there, the necessary steps are taken to fashion the imagined object out of some type of physical material in the three-dimensional space. And so the artist uses the imagination as the first step toward manifestation.

It is important to understand that it is the emotional frequency of an imagined object that leads the artist into an understanding of the following steps needed to create a physical manifestation of the imagined object. As such, it is this frequency of imagination that dictates manifestation; whether it be a physical object, an event, a circumstance, a relationship, or the outcome of some event. The highest frequency of imagination will cause feelings of anticipation, joy, and excitement. This frequency will be translated into some form of material space within the energy field of the individual, and it will then find those things that match that frequency and draw them into that energetic field.

This is the nature of all manifestations in the physical world, and they all begin within the energetic space of the imagination. There is much to be said for frequent daydreaming, deliberate and conscious visualizing, and even imagination that occurs in the dream state, as they all contain the frequency needed to create. And so we would like to emphasize that exercising one's imagination is one of the best ways to ensure that you are using your free will to create those things that you desire, rather than those things that you wish to avoid. It is quite simply an act of choosing what you wish to see in your life and focusing the enormous power of your imagination on that frequency, rather than on the frequency of that which you wish to eliminate, avoid, or release from your life.

As with any other sense, this sense of imagination needs to be used, experimented with, and controlled so that it is deliberately focused on desire, on an intuitive knowing, and on creating a sense of fulfillment and happiness in one's life. Those who spend a lot of time within their imagination, such as artists, writers, musicians, and actors, will find that creative process to be not only vital to their lives but also essential to their well-being. Artists will testify that there is much beauty that comes out of challenge, and much expression that comes out of emotional trauma. This is not to say that happy people cannot create, but that those who are able to manipulate the frequency of crisis through the imagination can find that much beauty can be found within it.

The imagination is one of your greatest sources of personal power, and we encourage you to work with it, utilize it, and create not only the material aspects of your life but the nonmaterial experiences, the sense of self, and the conditions that allow you to express the greatest gift of yourself to the world.

PLEASE EXPLAIN THE POWER OF PRAYER.

The power of prayer lies in the vibrational shift that occurs when one is in the state of consciousness that is achieved when one is intentionally acknowledging one's ever-present connection to Source. When one is in a state of prayer, one is activating that connection; as such, the aspect of the individual that *is* Source is also activated, altering the vibrational field of the individual and lending power to their intentions. Therefore, it is not in the asking for divine intervention that alterations are made to the individual's life path, but in the intrinsic power of Source energy within the individual that shifts the vibrational frequency from one of helplessness to powerful creator.

The assistance that is derived from prayer, therefore, is not exactly what many may think it is. When prayers are answered, one will naturally assume that the hand of God deemed the individual worthy for His benevolent power to release that individual from suffering. In fact, it is in the realization of one's *own power* to release himself from suffering that the true magic of prayer occurs. One cannot have a conversation with another being without activating the connection between them, whether this conversation is face-to-face or over long distances, and so, as a sort of vibrational conversation with Source, prayer activates this inherent connection and opens the channel to this direct link, calling in the vibrational frequency of the individual to the frequency of that which they are requesting. This is where prayer truly has an effect, when one is requesting a shift in the frequency of their life that will cause a healing, or a reconciliation, or a resolution. The act of prayer places the individual in the frequency of that which they are requesting, and so it is the supreme act of manifesting. It is a way to experience the energy of that which is being requested, turning it over to the infinite power of the divine, and then no longer dwelling in the frequency of helplessness, because the act of praying in itself is an act of creation.

There are, of course, as many different types of prayer as there are individuals, and so when one is involved in prayer that is an act of *dis*-connecting with the divine, one may find that these prayers feel quite empty and one may not experience much of a shift. For example, one can pray within the frequency of not deserving that which is being asked for, or feeling the need to earn the benevolence of the divine. This type of vibrational frequency actually pushes one out of resonance with one's connection to the divine, and while it can create some energetic shifts, the individual will never truly absolve herself of the perceived negative aspects of being, and will therefore block the vibrational shifts that could create an ease of her suffering. In other words, if one creates suffering as a form of identity, as a sense of deserved punishment, or as an inevitable outcome of being alive, one will probably not experience much relief from the act of prayer.

As with any type of energetic shift, the power of prayer can expand when performed in community with others. However, this does not mean that solitary prayer is less effective for an individual. It takes only a small amount of energy to create a ripple effect in the frequency of one's energy, and this can occur in many different ways. If many thousands of people are praying, they are, each one of them, activating their own personal connection to Source energy; so even when those prayers are directed toward another individual, the act of praying in itself is creating shifts in their own energy field that will create an influence on the energy of the person being prayed for. This is effective, but not as effective as the shift that occurs for one's *own* energy field in the act of praying. A person praying for herself is much more energetically powerful than many people praying for her could be. That does not mean that people shouldn't bother praying for others, it simply means that one's energetic influence on their own life's path is much greater than the influence of others. And so, when praying for others, it is important to keep in mind that your influence cannot overcome the energetic trajectory of the individual's life path; it can only support and uplift the vibrational field of the individual as an act of compassion and comfort. Your prayer, no matter where it is directed, serves mostly to alter your own vibrational field, thus influencing, but not necessarily altering, the frequency of others.

We would recommend that in all acts of prayer, one strive to open the channels of connection to the divine that are ever present, and in the act of feeling the energy of that connection, one create the sense of that which is in the highest and most divine aspect of being. In the act of asking for healing, one accesses one's own power to heal; in asking for forgiveness, one experiences the power of their own need to forgive; when asking for relief from suffering, one is open to a shift in perspective on the meaning of suffering. In this way, one is truly sitting in their own power as a co-creator and opening the channel of support and guidance from the highest aspect of the Divine Source within.

PLEASE EXPLAIN THE VIRTUES OF MEDITATION AND THE BEST WAY TO DEVELOP ITS PRACTICE, WHICH FOR MYSELF, AND FOR MANY PEOPLE I HEAR FROM, IS RATHER CHALLENGING AND SEEMINGLY FRUITLESS.

We would first advise that you cease "working" with meditation and that you begin to play with it. This does not have to be a serious, controlled, or even scheduled event in your day. In fact, in your case, we would advise against making this a separate part of your daily routine or beginning to see it as another form of work, since as you go about the business of meditation with the same energy as you go about your daily business of work, your mind will continue to function as though it were working, rather than in a state of peace, relaxation, and inner flow. It would appear that this is how you, specifically, are approaching this task, and we want to stress to you that this will not work. Meditation, if it is to be effective in any way, must come from a sense of inner flow, a sense of play, a sense of getting into a more natural state of being that allows one to go deeper and be within a state of the vibration of oneness, solitude, and divine quiet.

It would seem that your expectations around what this spiritual exploration should be bringing you may be blocking your ability to truly feel it in a natural state of flow. Spiritual experiences are often subtle shifts of energy that are barely discernible to the five senses, and others may only appear significant in hindsight.

We would like to stress that it is exactly in those times when you feel you do not have time for self-care that it is most needed. And we are feeling that practicing meditation has not worked so well for you because you are seeing it as just another item on your to-do list, rather than a sacred act.

If you are finding it difficult to fit a 20-minute meditation into your daily schedule, it may be a good idea to bring a sense of meditation into your day in small bits, rather than a 20-minute block of time. We suggest that you begin early in the morning, upon rising, to set intentions for what you would like to achieve in that day in the way of a higher connection, and that you intersperse the many activities in your day with small periods of quietude, either indoors or out, with the intention to quiet your mind and open your senses to that higher connection. If you are finding that stillness and sitting is not bringing you to the state you desire, we recommend that you bring the intention into your daily walks, into your short breaks from your desk, into time spent with your child, and into the moments before sleep. These are all meditative times, and bringing the intention to achieve a higher state of spiritual awareness into those things that you are already doing, rather than looking to change your schedule to "try" to find that connection, may create a better flow for you.

We also want to point out that the writing you do is mostly achieved through a type of meditative state; the consciousness that is needed to bring forth the wisdom that you share is that same state that one experiences in meditation. So when you are doing this type of work, we would define that state of consciousness as one of meditation.

Another issue that we feel you, and perhaps others, may be bumping up against in this endeavor is the need to control your external circumstances. While you are of a higher state of consciousness that understands the flow of universal energy, you are also in the awareness of the lack of so-called intelligence around you (made clear in your earlier questions) and a sense that there is much work to be done and not enough time to do it. This places you in the energy of one who must constantly be doing, rather than being in a more natural flow of allowing. And it is not just through a 20-minute meditation that you can achieve that state of beingness; it is in all the minutes of your day where you make the choice to focus on one thing or another, in napping, and in quiet contemplation. Bring the intention of ease into your day; find moments of simply being, rather than doing; catch your whirring mind and allow it to rest in brief moments of stillness; and perhaps be a bit more discerning about the people and things that pull you into their energy. This is where you will begin to release your grip on the need to direct the flow and move more easily into a sense of being *in* the flow.

HOW MUCH TIME DO YOU SPEND PER DAY (IF COMPARaBLE) IN MEDITATION AND PSYCHIC EXPLoRATIONS?

We have, in our daily waking lives, achieved a state of consciousness that no longer needs to practice meditation, as it is already part of the way we conduct our lives. You might say that we are in a constant state of meditation, and yet we are functioning quite deliberately through that higher conscious state. It is not what your religious scholars would define as enlightenment; however, it is the highest form of enlightened consciousness that we have been able to achieve to date. There may be moments when we feel the need to pull away from daily activities and retreat to a state of quiet and calm, but it does not take more than a brief time of that state of consciousness to clear the energy of whatever was misaligning us and return to the more balanced state.

The same answer applies to the exploration of the higher realms of energetic connection; as it is part of the way we live our lives, we no longer need to set aside time to focus completely on it as a practice. Our state of "being" is one of a natural connection with the divine, with each other, and with higher knowledge. We arrived there through different vehicles of meditation, energy work, healing the traumas of dissent among us, and coming into a greater sense of compassion and peace with ourselves and others.

HOW CAN WE AVOID DISASTERS? OR WIN THE LOTtERY? WHAT IS THE BEST WAY TO WARD OFf AND AVOID EXTREMELY STRANGE, UNUSUAL, OR PAINFUL (EMOTIONALLY AND PHYSICALLY) "ACCIDENTS" (OR UNINTENDED MANIFESTATIONS)? OF COURSE, EVERYTHING ADDS TO OUR GROWTH; TO BE CLEAR, THAT IS NOT THE QUESTION. FOR EXAMPLE: DYING IN A TERRORIST SHOOTING, WINNING THE LOTtERY, LOSING A CHILD, INVENTING A FAD/ TREND THAT TAKES THE WORLD BY STORM (LIKE THE HULA- HOOP OR IPHONE), ETC. DO SUCH EXTREME MANIFESTATIONS ONLY COME FROM EXTREME AND PERSISTENT THINKING?

This question contains some examples that may stem from a form of fate, a deliberate manifestation, or intention made in advance of the incarnation, confirmed in the moment of occurrence by the nonphysical aspect of the one involved. While it is true that the life path is determined largely by the choice-making and free will of the individual and their subsequent power of manifestation, there are other elements at work in the unfolding of one's path. The aspect of the soul that incarnates into the physical creates a sort of blueprint of that life path, which includes certain aspects that will best present opportunities for certain types of learning, growth, and experience. As such, the individual is able to respond to those life circumstances using free will in such a way that will optimize those experiences or be victimized by them. Challenging situations serve a higher purpose that extends beyond any pain or suffering that ensues in the earthly experience; it is what the individual does to respond to those circumstances that creates the path to unfold before them. And if that path includes the opportunity or probability of what may be judged as an untimely, violent, or otherwise disturbing demise, please be assured that the aspect of the soul that chose that particular incarnation has agreed to that demise, and it has not experienced the loss of its life as something that was beyond its control, no matter how that death appears to the outside world.

It is true that all life experiences contain probabilities and possibilities that are activated or defused by the choices of the will, but it is also true that all the possibilities are part of the agreement made at the time of the incarnation. And so, if one has the probability of an early death, or perhaps a severe injury or some other kind of suffering, it is not the case that that circumstance was forced upon the incarnate being without the permission of the soul being. All roles played out in the life of the incarnate being are roles that have been partly written before the spirit matter becomes physical, and while the outcomes of these roles have an infinite number of possibilities based on the responses of the incarnate being to their circumstances, the spirit has decided in advance that her best chance of soul evolution lies within those possibilities, and so the soul agrees to anything that may happen to it while in the physical life.

This means that someone who is murdered by a terrorist, as well as the terrorist himself, have agreed to partake of these roles as part of their life's path in this lifetime. Of course, the outcome of these life paths is not inevitable; the victim may "accidentally" miss a flight, or be delayed or held back from the experience in some way that will alter their course. The terrorist may change his mind, come to his senses and decide he isn't able to complete his task, or may manifest a faulty weapon. In both cases, the possibilities have been considered and each soul has decided in advance that they will play out these roles not only for the enrichment of their own lives, but for the repercussions that are then felt by all involved in these circumstances, who would have similarly chosen their participation, even if these repercussions are deemed to be painful and full of grief.

This is quite a difficult concept to understand when one is in the physical, as one will have an instinctual desire to avoid painful and negative situations, and will perceive untimely death as a great tragedy—and in many ways this is correct. But when one is able to gain the perspective that can only be achieved through the transition or otherwise delving into the nonphysical, one will be able to perceive the many gifts afforded in these circumstances and the aspects of pain that can enrich the experience of the soul being. Understand that some soul beings have agreed to a life of extremes; they may be those who experience great fame, wealth, illness, physical or mental challenges, loss, or poverty. And there are those who choose a more subtle life experience that affords a more contemplative life path. No choice is judged as better than any other, and no action is judged as wrong or right; it is only the ego mind of the physically manifested being that can form these judgments. Therefore, it is only in the mind of the incarnate being that the idea of suffering and pain can exist.

Therefore, to seek to avoid any circumstances that may lead to tragedy, pain, or death in the daily experience of the individual is an instinctual desire, but to dwell on these things only incites a fear of living. It is true that the amnesia that occurs when one transitions into a physical body means that one is never fully aware of what may occur in their life's path, but it is also true that the soul aspect of the being is fully aware of these possibilities and agrees to incarnate anyway because the value of the enrichment and karmic identity that is afforded by these circumstances far outweighs the temporary nature of the pain and suffering that can be the result of them.

This is by no means a natural way of thinking when one is in the physical, and so it is something you may need to accept on faith as the truth. Death is not the tragedy that it appears to be, and the soul being does not carry with it any memory of suffering.

All pain is temporary, and death, in whatever way it occurs, is a peaceful and beautiful experience for the soul as it transitions to its natural state. When death is sudden and violent, the soul is assisted in that transition so that it is nurtured and carried into the peaceful state of nonphysical being.

We would once again like to stress that the value of any life is not measured by its length; as such, the life of a child that is seemingly cut short holds great value to all who have come into contact with that child, no matter how briefly that life was present. There is a rightness in all experiences, even those that you wish to avoid. And it is in the act of deliberate avoidance that one sometimes misses out on the joys of living free from worry and fear. Faith in the trajectory of your life's path, deliberate focus on that which creates joy and happiness, and a sense of love in all you do will help to alleviate those fears and will help you see that you are eternally loved and supported by the universe, even when it appears that you are in a state of suffering and grief.

DOES THE WORK THAT YOU DO—THAT I DO—REALLY MAKE A DIFFERENCE?

Ah, this is a question that we often ask of ourselves, and it has always become clear through the exploration of our work that it most certainly does. It is the universal call to the soul of those of us who are conscious enough to heed it. It is the destiny and purpose of those who are tuned in to the universal field of knowledge to assist others in their quest for a deeper connection with themselves and Source. It is not work in the conventional definition of the word; it is joy, it is an irresistible urge, it is a sense of destiny that cannot be denied by those who sense it, and it is this sensation that resonates with the truth of that which we are driven to share, driven enough to project ourselves through vast reaches of space and time, altering the very fabric of the universe to promulgate. Assisting others to embrace these concepts is the highest calling of the universe. How could it NOT make a difference?

RESPONSIBILITY IS A BIG WORD THAT GETS USED A LOT, PAR-
TICULARLY IN SPIRITUALLY MINDED CIRCLES; MANY OF US HAVE
LONG BEEN TOLD THAT WE SHOULD PUT THE NEEDS OF OTHERS
BEFORE OUR OWN. ARE WE *RESPONSIBLE* FOR EACH OTHER, AS A
RACE AND AS A SPECIES?

When it comes to taking charge of one's own life and using one's energy wisely, there's a negative tone to this word that often leads to its avoidance. People will even create an atmosphere of victimhood and blame to absolve themselves of what they believe to be their responsibilities to their own happiness and peace of mind. If one is at the mercy of the reactions or actions of others, one no longer needs to feel responsibility to oneself, as one will not feel in control of their emotional and mental state. This negates the heavy energy of responsibility, and when this method of living becomes habitual, there is a great deal of comfort to be found in it, even when this comfort is surrounded by misery.

There is such a thing as joyous responsibility, however, and we would like to suggest that one seek to express joy in the actions that one does out of a sense of responsibility. There is a great deal of satisfaction to be found in taking charge of one's own life and removing control from other individuals, events, and circumstances of one's life. The resulting freedom to choose one's own life path and no longer be bound to the whims and desires of others is one of life's greatest joys, and one that we highly recommend.

The sense of responsibility to others can also take on a joyful tone when it is viewed through the lens of compassionate service. When one is centered in a heart space of compassion and love, any actions toward others will always be done with a sense of alignment with one's true purpose, which in large part is to be of service to others and to shine one's light upon the world in such a way that it uplifts those around them.

While it is true that some responsibilities weigh heavier than others, understand that it is your attitude about them that will cause them to feel either burdensome or like just another form of joyous self-expression. When one is feeling burdened by responsibility, it is important to assess the situation to see if a different relationship can be formed with it, or if one simply needs to request more help if the sense of responsibility is too much for one person to bear.

It is also important to note that it is never your responsibility to change, fix, or heal another person. Caring for others is an act of support, love, and compassion. It seeks to simply validate the existence of another through kindness and consideration, without judgment or condemnation for their choices. Caring for others from the heart is a true act of divine love; this will only become burdensome when one allows judgment, criticism, or a feeling that one is not being appreciated to enter the process. We would suggest that feelings of resentment can be examined to find their true origin and that a different perspective can be chosen when this feeling arises.

We are each responsible for the energy we emit; we are responsible for the care and compassion that we show to ourselves and to others; we are not responsible to all people all the time; and we are not responsible for fixing the planet or the universe. Do your own part with a sense of joy and gratitude, and the world will take care of fixing itself as it is supported through the energy of these acts of kindness.

SHOULD THIS INFORMATION BE GIVEN AWAY FOR FREE?

It is our desire that the information and exercises put forth in these sessions be viewed as valuable bits of wisdom that are being brought forth through the efforts and talents of those involved, namely Tracy, Mike, and others involved in its distribution. While we no longer participate in a monetary exchange in our world, we understand the energetic value that is placed on those things for which an exchange is made, and so we fully support the need to charge accordingly. There is a great deal of time and energy going into the planning and preparation of such creations, and so this exchange not only equalizes that energetic output, it assists those who participate in their understanding of the value to their lives that is being received. Even in those systems that do not include a monetary exchange, there is some other type of energetic exchange that recognizes value; whenever one's talents, labor, and time are offered, there is an understanding that the value of that energy will be returned at some point through a similar offering made to them when it is needed. In your current system, these checks and balances are made in the form of the concept of currency, which is simply a placeholder for energy owed. Understand that even when something is presented as a gift or as a free service, there is some type of energetic reciprocation. When time and energy are not reciprocated, their value is often underestimated and unappreciated, as the cycle of energetic flow is left incomplete. Therefore, we find the appropriate fees being charged are quite acceptable in exchange for what we have to offer and the time and energy put into producing these offerings.

WHAT MAY WE ALl ASPIRE TO IN TERMS OF ENLIGHTENMENT?

We have observed many in your world who operate with the belief that enlightenment is the ultimate goal of any spiritual path, and in fact, the ultimate experience of existence in any form. It is this belief system that causes many visual depictions of enlightenment as being discovered on a mountaintop, or available only to the most disciplined yogis or spiritual masters. It is often seen as an unattainable miracle of awareness, an epiphany of the highest form of spiritual awakening, and available to a select few who dedicate their lives to the pursuit of it. It is, in this sense, the final destination that will lead to oneness with Source.

We would like to call hogwash on these notions.

Instead, we would like to suggest to you that enlightenment is a continual state of being; it is what leads us to a daily sense of self-discovery, of self-examination and inner inquiry. It is a journey that never ends, both in the physical and nonphysical realms. It is not a destination, it is the journey itself. With every joy, every conflict, every pain, and every triumph comes another opportunity for discovering an aspect of enlightened being. Each and every experience you encounter on the physical plane offers the chance to shed light on yourself and your existence; the way that you respond to these experiences will dictate how you choose to experience that light. As such, the term *enlightenment* can be seen as a continual string of lights that are illuminated every time you learn about another aspect of your being, whether it is physical, intellectual, spiritual, emotional, or supremely mystical. Enlightenment can be found in the simplest, most mundane aspects of being imaginable. It can be experienced in the day-to-day encounters, in the quiet solitude of your morning commute, in the deep conversations with a friend, in the ecstatic union of lovers, and it is usually NOT a conscious experience of oneness with the divine. It is a light that is shed on an inner knowing, it is a subconscious moment of inner resonance with truth, it is an innate sense of being exactly where you need to be at any given moment—and those levels of conscious experience can be overshadowed by the constant monologue of the mind that is focused on the falsehoods of a learned belief system.

Your being is perpetually benefiting from these small moments of enlightenment; in fact, these moments are among the reasons you chose to experience this lifetime in the way that you have structured it. Each tiny light that is lit in the spirit being, in the deeper knowing of the soul, in the quiet recesses of consciousness, adds to the overall light of the complete soul being and sheds a bit more understanding of the nature of the divine and the universal laws of consciousness. Even if you are not consciously aware of them, these moments offer a priceless series of lessons into the nature of being on levels that reach beyond the power of your physical brain.

And so, we would suggest that you cease your search for the supreme experience of enlightenment as the goal of your existence. We would suggest that the Buddha's experience under the Bodhi tree was merely an epiphany of spirit, a connection of his will with that of the divine, and that it was not the end of his spiritual journey but just the beginning, as it is for anyone who feels the calling to an inner examination of consciousness through an expansion of their energy toward the divine.

Enlightenment, then, will come when you cease striving for it. It will come as you stare into your coffee cup, it will come when you hug your child, it will come when you make a deadline or argue with a friend. It will come whether your conscious mind acknowledges it or not, and it will sometimes culminate in a huge spiritual epiphany, and it is in those moments of clarity that a new journey begins.

WHAT ARE 10 SUGGESTIONS FOR US TO ACCOMPLISH OUR SOULS' LIFE OBJECTIVE(S)?

As we've discussed, you decided to incarnate in this place in time to fulfill certain missions of learning and enrichment of your soul. The blueprint of your life's path has been set up in such a way to best support the types of learning that you have decided were best for the evolution of your soul being and the enhancement of your spirit. Not all of these missions will necessarily be accomplished, however, due to an inability to overcome some challenges or a disposition that fails to focus on them. Here are some ways to ensure that the choices you are making are in the best interest of your soul's purpose:

1. **Listen to Your Intuition, or Inner Voice.**
   This voice is the direct line of communication to your higher self, or your soul self, which holds the knowledge about who you really are and why you are here. This knowledge will not be completely accessible to your conscious mind; however, by listening to the subtle cues and signals of your intuitive voice, you will find that you are guided into the choices of action that will best serve the purpose of your incarnation. This intuitive self is also a direct link to divine wisdom, and so practicing and strengthening your intuitive self is a great way to become more confident with your abilities and more comfortable with yourself in general. The more confidence you have in your choice-making, the more you are able to use these choices in your best interest and not blame others for the outcome of

these choices. Your intuition will be the voice of your inner passions, desires, and gifts; it will hold the key to the type of action that will bring you the most fulfillment and sense of purpose in this lifetime. It will send you subtle and encouraging urges and cues that will signal when it is time to make a change, move forward with an intention, or rest. Learning to pay attention to this inner voice is one of the best ways to discern your purpose, allow yourself to be guided by your inner longings, and give yourself permission to feel whatever it is that you need to feel.

2. **Embrace and Honor Your Talents and Gifts.** If you don't believe you have any, go back to your childhood. What did you love to do? What absorbed your attention and kept you occupied for hours on end? What feels like it is the genuine expression of your soul's work? If you already have a passion in your life, how are you expressing it? Is there something like fear or self-consciousness that is holding you back from the expression of your true self? Do you feel the need to fit the cultural conditioning that states that only those talents and gifts that can earn money or land you long-term employment are worthy of expression?

3. **Find the Lessons and Gifts in All Experiences.** In order to truly embrace the path that you have chosen for this incarnation, it is important that you understand that each and every day offers gifts of learning, growth, and evolution, and that it is not only in the major life epiphanies and challenges that learning occurs. Even the most mundane of days offers gifts if you choose to see them. Be alert and present in every experience, from daily chores, errands, and conversations to big decisions, crises,

CHANNELED MESSAGES from DEEP SPACE

and disagreements, for that is where you will find
the greatest reflections of your own true self and
universal guidance on your life's path. If you are, at
any time, feeling an urge to make a change or find
a higher path, listen to the urge and investigate the
implications of it. Often the universe will create a
sense of disquietude or dissatisfaction in your present
position so that you are motivated to continue
forward.

4. **Write and/or Journal.** Expressing your innermost
feelings, thoughts, and desires in a diary or journal
is an excellent way to get better in touch with your
true authentic self and to understand where some
of these seemingly unusual urges are originating.
Keeping track of the events in your life and how
they coincide with your thought patterns also helps
you to understand the influence of the energy of
your thoughts on your external life. Writing also
helps you keep in touch with your inner life in quite
a creative way, and so you are helping to move the
energy forward by releasing some pent-up feelings or
frustrations on paper before they can manifest in a
regrettable way. We suggest that you write down your
dreams, hopes, and desires, along with your greatest
attributes, skills, and talents. See if you can read
your entries back in a sort of detached way. What
would you think of this person? What type of self-
expression would be best for this person?

5. **Be Gentle with Yourself.** See mistakes and so-
called wrong turns simply as ways to address what
brought you to that place. No choice of relationship,
job, or material gain is going to be enough to take
you on to the next leg of this life's journey. It is what
you choose to learn from these experiences that will

guide you, and so you can let yourself off the hook for having to do everything perfectly "right" all the time. You simply cannot make a "wrong" choice, since within every choice is a set of potentials. These potentials may include many starts and stops, many redirections, disappointments, and exciting beginnings. This is the journey you envisioned at the time you decided to map out your present incarnation; the desire for things to be easy and to avoid missteps comes from misplaced expectations about what your life is meant to be. Allow yourself to fall, but be vigilant in seeing the value in what you deem to be failure, as this is where you will truly grow and ascend, should you allow it.

6. **Avoid Comparison.** As you navigate the constantly changing tides of your journey, it will often appear to you that others have it easier, or that they are better at steering their ships. Understand that this is often a fallacy, and that you are basing this assumption purely on the projection of your own desires and what you see on the outer surface of their situation. No being who incarnates into the physical is without a certain amount of challenge, struggle, and misfortune, as it is within those very difficult circumstances that their true nature is able to shine and their divine will can be exercised to make the choices that will allow for their spirit's ascension. Without these missteps and challenges, the experience would be an empty one, and there would be little need to go to the trouble of being in this state of existence. You came here to be challenged, to continually rise above any adversity, to exercise your divinity in countless ways every day that you exist. Your influence on others is not limited to those times

of great success; in fact, it is in those times of rising above what you deem as failure that you most inspire those around you. Setting standards or expectations based on what you think others are doing is greatly limiting your own experience, and only believing what you see is limiting the depth of your vision.

7. **Have Fun.** While there is a serious nature to the work of being an incarnated being in the physical world, we would like to challenge the notion that those activities that are purely playful or simply for the pure pleasure of the individual are trivial, unimportant, or unnecessary. A sense of joyful expression through play and leisure, laughter and expressions of delight, sensual pleasures and physical bliss, are all highly important aspects of being. The energy of these acts is not only a huge component of this state of being, it inspires and accelerates the movement of all other types of expressive energy, which is vital to the evolution of your planet as a whole. Without the experience of delight, rapture, and joy, what motivation is there to accomplish anything? Do not negate the power of a good laugh, the satiation of a good meal, or the physical delights of love. These experiences are not only gifts to you, they are designed to create a collective consciousness of gratitude and value to this incarnate experience that is so much greater than any of the challenges also inherent in it. We would recommend that you enjoy all the aspects of this time you have as a physical being as much as possible.

8. **Do Not Follow the Beaten Path.** Even if your life's trajectory takes you on a somewhat traditional path of education and career, find ways to be an innovator, to stretch boundaries, and challenge

well-worn systems. Do not fear retribution for questioning authority or suggesting new perspectives. It is only in daring to be the one who creates change, rather than the one who dutifully performs the robotic tasks of an uninspired life, that advances can be made both personally and universally. We would suggest that you do not shrink from the possibility of criticism or derision; very few people are willing to see the value of fresh perspectives and change, and so they will resist it through ridicule and disdain. Trust your intuition to know when change is needed or when minds need to be opened to new systems, and push past the fear of judgment, as this is where the true innovators, inventors, radical thinkers, and spiritual leaders have been leading the way to an advancement of culture, science, and social systems. And not all leaders will be found in the spotlight.

9. **Do Not Be Afraid to Ask for Help.** While it is true that your life's journey is an individual one, the idea of a collective consciousness dictates the need for cooperative acts of creation. It is a natural tendency of the incarnated being to want to be of service; as such, the simple act of asking for help can provide another with a sense of purpose, a joy of being, and the fulfillment of destiny that can cause huge shifts in energy. Asking for assistance is affirming the value of another, and it is creating a combined force of energy that has the ability to shift from the act of struggling to the ease of the collective. There is much to be said about the power of energy that is joined toward a common intention; the sum of that energy is much greater than its parts, and so the act of reaching out to others creates a oneness of purpose and a collective of individual gifts and talents all

directed toward a similar path. Find those with whom you most resonate energetically, and you will find the power of that collective force to be one that can create without limitations.

10. **Ensure That Love Is Part of All You Do.** Every act that has the energy of love brought into it is strengthened, enhanced, and made divine in all its aspects. This includes even those things that do not appear to have any connection to the feeling or aspect of love with which you are usually acquainted. It may seem a bit strange to perform everyday, mundane tasks with love, but there is a sense of magic that is created there that is only possible through heart-centered and love-focused action. This love is not limited to the romantic partnership type of love that you may normally associate with the idea of the concept, nor is it limited to the friends and family that you hold dear. It is the love of oneself, the love of the life you are experiencing in all its aspects; it is the love of spirit expressed in all forms of physical matter; it is the love of the Creator, or divine will, which is expressed through you at all times. There is no limit to the ways that this love can be expressed in your world; experiment with new ways to expand and deliver this love in all reaches of your energy's scope, as this is what is at the core of your being and the heart of your existence in all its forms.

HOW CAN WE WORK WITH THE ENERGETIC SHIFTS TAKING PLACE UPON OUR PLANET TO BUILD A BETTER WORLD?

As discussed earlier, the energy of your Earth during our conversations with you has been quite intense, and some of the more dramatic fluctuations of this energy have been felt in a challenging way among those of you who work with energy on a regular basis. The cosmic shifts that are involved in these energetic fluctuations are amassed around some intense solar activity and some fluctuating magnetic and gravitational forces that, while subtle as measured by scientific instruments, are felt in quite a strong way in the energy fields of all people on your planet. While these shifts are not always felt on a conscious level, they are deeply felt within other layers of consciousness, and can be found to disrupt sleep and cause some emotional disturbances for the more sensitive among you.

As we stated previously, these fluctuations are all part of the larger energetic shift that has been present for quite a while on your planet, and so in the long run, these pulses of strong, unusual energy will be what initiate many of the shifts in consciousness among your people. These shifts will then lead to the changes that your planet is heading toward, and the possibilities that are available through these changes are quite remarkable. You are already beginning to see some of the effects of these energy fluctuations in some of the recent worldwide events.

There are among you many who are finding an irrepressible urge to speak out against some of the corrupt and failing systems that dominate your planet, and it is these souls who are feeling the most dominant aspects of the shift, which is to spur people into action and to ignite a passionate need for higher consciousness living. These individuals will be the ones who help to usher in the new age, which will be shifting toward the oneness concept and the downfall of rampant consumerism and corrupt leadership.

While these energies may feel quite strong and overwhelming at this time, it is through this energy that a softening can occur among your peoples: a sense of gentler compassion and a need for the disintegration of the walls that separate each individual from the other. It is time for the acknowledgment of oneness among all people, and the feeling of stewardship and responsibility for all living beings and ecological systems. Through this stronger connection with all that is on your planet will come new, more environmentally harmonious systems that will usher in a new age unlike any other you have experienced.

Another aspect to this shift in consciousness is a higher connection to the spirit self, to spirit energy, and to divine energy. This connection may present some brief challenges for some among you, but eventually, those who choose to pursue it will see the magic inherent in this connection and will find great peace is gleaned from it. Those who do not wish to participate in this aspect of their higher vibrational attunement will find other outlets for this energy, which may include more earthly pursuits such as musical and artistic endeavors. In every case, there is a great bliss to be bestowed upon all who find themselves shifting into a higher state of consciousness.

Among those who are awakening will arise several new leaders, some of whom will become very prominent outside of the normal realm of politics, but who will have great influence nonetheless. These new leaders will be identified by their penchant for the truth and a need for peaceful solutions to world conflict. They will suggest new systems that may at first be scoffed at by those who resist change, but will find growing support among those who see the merits and necessity of these changes. Understand that while the political figures who are arising at this time have limited influence, new types of leadership will begin to emerge that will find other ways to influence the trajectory of your societal systems and motivate others to create their own systems within their neighborhoods and towns. There will be small uprisings that will challenge the political systems and begin to disintegrate some of the old systems in favor of new types of leadership. Again, this will start small but will grow exponentially within a short period of time.

Many changes will occur imminently on your planet (certainly within the next few years), but they will be changes that appear to be quite subtle at first. As their supporters grow in number, the systems of power that are now so unbalanced in your world will begin to be shaken up, and the largest conglomerates of business and industry will feel their power weaken.

This is not meant to be a fearful time, although there will be many among you who will advocate fear, since this is a typical response to change. And so it is crucial that those of you who understand the need for these changes be the calm center of the storm, and that you maintain your well-cultivated centers of peaceful response to the challenges that will be posed. The role of each and every person who is practicing methods of higher consciousness will be quite important, even if you don't recognize yourself as a leader in the traditional sense of the word. Never underestimate the power of your energy to lead others into a more beneficial mode of thinking.

Whenever you find yourself facing a milestone such as a new year, a birthday, or any type of life transition, it is a good time to take stock of your life and all you have accomplished so far. We wish you to focus on all that you have overcome and risen above throughout your lives, and understand that you are here in this time of great flux on purpose; it was your highest choice to participate in this crucial time, and even the smallest action toward a brighter future will have great consequence. Remember your methods for maintaining a sense of deliberate and purposeful creation with your thoughts and attitudes, and continue to monitor your responses to some of the challenges that lie ahead. There are none that cannot be overcome and in fact, none that do not offer the opportunity for great advancement for all of your people.

For now, we wish you to focus your attention on those things that bring you great joy, and feel that joy as you anticipate what is to come, as it is the ushering in of a new age among all the beings of your planet, and it is a great privilege to be among those beings who will benefit from these shifts and see the potential for all that is to come. We are quite honored to be among you at this time.

PART 5

ASKING
BETTER
QUESTIONS

Throughout the formulation of all I
asked Frank, I was mindfully aware
of the old adage: "There are things
you know you know. And there are
things you know you don't know. But
it's the things you don't know that you
don't know that you have to be careful
about." Not being able to get out of my
own head and see the shortcomings to
my line of questioning, I thought I'd
offer some catchall questions—asking
Frank what else I should be asking—
in an effort to leave no stone
unturned in our quest to ultimately
share some of their lofty worldviews.

WHAT 10 QUESTIONS WOULD I BE WISE TO ASK YOU AND HOW WOULD YOU ANSWER THEM?

Above all, we would like you to understand that the reason for our presence among you is the desire to help guide and support your innate power to create, to manifest, and to direct the course of your own individual lives and, in turn, the trajectory of your planet's future. We do not claim to have all the answers for you, nor can we predict the future for you or your planet; instead, we wish to demonstrate to you how this future is as malleable as clay in your own hands, and that it is through your own power of discernment, wise choice-making, forward-thinking creation, and connection with divine knowledge that will be the catalyst for an amazing, rich, and fruitful existence for each and every one of you and for the collective whole. As such, these are the questions we hope to inspire in you:

1. HOW CAN I BEST HARNESS MY INnATE, DIVINE WILl AND POWER TO CREATE THE LIFE THAT I DESIRE, BOTH INDIVIDU-ALlY AND AS A COLlECTIVE CONSCIOUSNEsS WITH ALl MY FELlOW HUMANS?

In order to harness any power, it is essential that you are first aware of it. Acknowledgment of your divinity is an important component of connecting with the aspect of yourself that is a powerful creative force, capable of far more than you may imagine. As a physical being with a logical mind, it is important to you to have hard evidence of any belief before you will adopt it as truth, and so it is a valuable exercise to scan your past for evidence of your power as the manifester of your life circumstances. Can you find instances, events, and circumstances where there is no doubt that your desires were answered by the force of the universe in an uncanny way? Can you see how you have created your life up to the present moment? Can you look at the circumstances that challenged you and realize that it was your response to those circumstances that led you through them and created a new path that may be even better for your present life circumstances?

As you acknowledge this power, you will begin to understand that even when it is used in an unconscious way, it is a magnificent force, and so it would stand to reason that when you now choose to deliberately and intentionally go about creating that which you desire, the same forces will pull together to bring these desires into your physical reality. If you can get to the point where you can witness this with wonder and delight, and can find a way to have fun with it, then the energy will flow freely without the obstruction of your doubts and disbelief.

Through the process of joyful creation, you will find that you can apply this energy to all the situations of your life, and that you can release many of the illusions that have been made manifest in your consciousness throughout your life, mostly by the well-meaning aims of others who were taught in the same way. It is through this deliberate choice-making that you may instill different truths and different ways of seeing the world that will allow you to create a new sense of your power within creation, and no longer feel as though you are simply a cog in the wheel or a victim of circumstance. Seeing past these illusions can create a sense of delight and self-confidence that will transmute many of your current struggles and conflicts into life-affirming challenges, and other opportunities to demonstrate your ability to rise above and enrich yourself through them.

While the power of any given individual is incredibly strong, the power of the collective is *infinitely* stronger, and so it is in the knowledge of this collective force that you can begin to see what needs to be done to direct the current changes in your world toward that which is in the highest good of all your planet's inhabitants and the planet itself. The coming together of even a small group of people who have common intentions greatly increases the energetic frequency of creation, and if you find yourself called to create such a community as a leader or teacher, you will find that this energy grows exponentially, even if you do not see the effects of that energy immediately. Have faith in the power of divine will to create that which is in the greatest good of all, and never fail to pull into your energetic circle those who are resonating with your own frequency of intent, for that is what will move the mountains currently in the way of your planet's progress.

2. HOW DO I OVERCOME THE YEARS OF DEePLY INGRAINED BELIEFS THAT TELl ME I AM POWERLESs, A VICTIM OF SOCIETY AND THE WILl OF BOTH THE UNSEeN AND THE POWERFUL LEADERS IN MY WoRLD?

Again, it is the awareness of these beliefs that is the first vital step toward altering them. When one refers to the unconscious state of the majority of your population, it is actually this state of unawareness that is being referred to; it is the unawareness of the origin of their so-called opinions and life philosophies as being something that has the potential to be misguided or flawed. It is the lack of understanding about how these beliefs are choices, and that one has the ability, power, and presence to create a new belief system, a new truth, a new philosophy that can be much more resonant with the desires and aims of the soul.

When it is observed within the thought process that an undesirable or negative thought is churning in one's mind, it is important to first become aware of and observe this thought from the perspective of an outsider, as though one were watching this thought emerge on a screen or on the page of a book. This sort of detached observation can help move the energy past any emotional attachment to the thought and prevent a cycle of negative thinking that may arise from it.

Once the thought is observed, one can choose to continue to engage in that thought as though it were truth, or question the thought and its value to the well-being of the individual. This is where the power of intention can be made manifest. If one has a clear intention of self-improvement and a move toward a more deliberate participation in the creation of one's life, the thought can then be put to the test against that intention. In other words, one may ask, "Is this thought resonant with my intention? Does this thought further the aims of this intention?" Then, through the process of choice, one may choose to replace the thought with one that feels more in line with what one wishes to create.

While this process may seem cumbersome at first, it is quite similar to the process of meditation, in which one chooses whether or not to engage in the intrusive thoughts that appear when in a state of quiet repose. If a thought appears during this meditative space, it is the choice of whether or not to engage in that thought that creates or disturbs the meditative state. Similarly, it is the choice of whether to engage in a thought that reflects a limited truth, thereby reinforcing that truth and preventing progress, or to disengage from that thought and choose a different, more expansive truth, which will dictate the success of one's trajectory toward their intentions for fulfillment and happiness.

As a step-by-step process, since we understand how helpful this can be to the logical mind, we would suggest that you:

1. Set a clear intention for what it is that you would like to attain, accomplish, or evolve into.

2. Create a habit of observing and listening to the thoughts that seem to randomly appear in your consciousness when you are not distracted by focused activity.

3. Deliberately and carefully allow yourself to detach from the thought, as though it were occurring outside your normal field of consciousness, thereby allowing a less emotional response to the thought.

4. Ask yourself whether this thought is resonant with the intentions you have set, or if it is creating a block to those intentions.

5. If it is determined that this is a thought that is perpetuating an unwanted truth, deliberately and consciously choose a different truth that is more resonant with your intention, more resonant with the truth of your soul, and more resonant with

the energy you would like to be experiencing and outwardly projecting.

6. Repeat, repeat, repeat.

Understand that this is a process, that while you will continue to grow, evolve, and expand through this process, you will always find new ways to apply it and you will continually be faced with new challenges to allow for this continued evolution and expansion. As such, it is important that you apply a certain amount of patience and gentle consolation to yourself through the process, and that you frequently remind yourself how far you have come through its application so that you do not get caught in a cycle of frustration or self-pity as you continue to discover new ways to apply it.

3. WHAT IS THE BEST WAY TO FEEL AND EXPERIENCE MY DIRECT CONNECTION TO THE DIVINE? IS IT POSSIBLE TO EXPERIENCE THE GOD PRESENCE IN MY LIFE?

Here again, awareness is the key to experiencing the divine presence in your day-to-day existence. Whether you have a religious background or not, you are taught from a very young age through imagery, language, and culture that the God presence is one that is outside the human experience. It is projected onto your consciousness as an unattainable connection, reached only through the act of death and touched upon through the supplication of prayer and worship. The energy of the Divine Spirit is often taught as one of judgment, of vengefulness, as one of a sort of jealous hoarding of supreme power. With this type of belief system accepted as divine truth, it will be quite difficult to truly feel a connection with one's own divine power and understand the inherent connection between the aspect of the spirit and Source.

Understand that because you are experiencing your incarnated state of being as one that is individual and separate from any and all other energies, you will tend to place these other energies into a hierarchy of separation. In other words, you will find those individuals with whom your energy most resonates, and that creates a sense of bonded connection, helping you to feel less isolated and misunderstood. Then there will be those whom you label as "others," for whom you may have some sense of compassion but not necessarily understand, and so you may find yourself critical or judgmental of their actions and thinking. Then there will be the "others" whom you place in a field of authority or a sense of achievement or attainment that you believe is beyond your scope of possibility, and so you may also find yourself critical, envious, or reverential of them.

What we would like to point out is that all of these "others" are connected to your energy in such a way that true separation is not possible, and that every being you encounter in your journey offers a certain reflection of an aspect of yourself, which may or may not be realized. While it is quite true that you are a unique and divine individual with your own inimitable combination of will, personality, and spirit, you are intrinsically connected, both through your human lineage and your soul energy, to every other being in existence, whether they are incarnate or not. And each and every being in existence, whether physical or nonphysical, is innately connected to, an embodiment of, and a conduit for Source energy.

Thus, the sense of disconnection from God, Source, or divine intelligence is an illusion that allows you to experience your incarnate journey in a particular way, with free will, independent choice-making, and conscious awareness. The influen and effect on your conscious awareness of the constant flow of energy from all other beings is not something you can feel or sense in the realm of your day-to-day existence, since you are focused on your own individual thoughts, beliefs, and sense-based experiences. However, this influence is palpable and can even be seen as waves and streams of energy by those in the nonphysical and by beings whose awareness allows such visual representations of energy.

With even the most basic awareness of how energy works, how it affects you, and how powerful the energy of your being is, you may be able to move beyond the limiting truth of your five senses and begin to understand the intrinsic energetic connection between yourself and others. And if you can begin to feel that connection, even in just the vaguest bit of awareness, it is possible that you may begin to understand that all aspects of your being reflect the awareness of the divine.

We would suggest, then, that you go out into the world holding this awareness in your conscious state of being. That is, simply assume for a moment that you are the embodiment of the divine, that Source is experiencing existence through your awareness of it; it is seeing the world through your eyes, hearing through your ears, feeling through your physical body and emotions. Imagine that at any given moment, the energy of the divine is flowing through your physical body, through the essence of your spirit being, and that it is ever present in every nuance of your being. See how this knowledge sharpens your focus on the external world, creates a different experience of that which you observe with your five senses, and that which you know through the essence of your energetic being. What does a flower look like through the eyes of the divine? How does Source hear the music on your radio or the chirping of a bird? How does God experience the energy of others?

Here is the challenge. It is to acknowledge yourself as the embodiment of not only your own unique and irreplaceable persona, but as the embodiment of all others, all being, all matter, and all consciousness, which, by definition, *is* the essence of Source energy.

4. HOW DO I FORGIVE, ACCEPT, AND EVEN LOVE THAT WHICH I SEE AS EVIL, REPREHENSIBLE, OR DELIBERATELY HURTFUL BEHAVIOR OF OTHERS? HOW DO I MINE TREASURE FROM THAT WHICH CHALLENGES ME TO THE POINT OF RAGE OR GRIEF?

First and foremost, you must set a clear intention for what you would like to achieve, which is peace of mind. It is in the acknowledgment that this peace of mind is paramount and is within your power to create that you begin to shift your desire for happiness away from being dependent on the behavior of others and back to your internal responses.

That being said, you must also be aware that there can be many different emotional triggers that occur when you encounter behavior from someone that you deem to be hurtful, dismissive, or neglectful. These triggers can connect to past experiences where you felt the same emotions; there can be childhood traumas or other distinct conflicts or crises that are unresolved in your consciousness, and when you begin to perceive that these emotional reactions are repeating, you may respond in an exaggerated way as those old, stored reactions struggle for release. It is true that emotions that are not dealt with in a timely manner will become locked in the physical body in such a way that they may create not only physical pain, illness, or disease, but also inflamed emotional pain that, when triggered, can result in outbursts of rage or extreme sadness. While these outbursts can be helpful to the physical body in the release of toxic stored emotions, they can also be harmful to relationships, so it is clear that your response to behavior from others that challenges you is best dealt with and released promptly.

As you begin to understand that your peace of mind is entirely up to you, you will find that you will no longer hold on to the feelings of hurt and dismay over the behavior of others for long periods of time. While you may find there is an initial emotional reaction, such as anger or sadness, your strong intention for peace of mind and your willingness to take on the responsibility for your own happiness will cause you to more quickly release these emotions and you will no longer suffer over them for long periods of time.

In addition to setting clear intentions, we suggest that you remind yourself that others' perception of the world and their place in it can never be the same as yours. While it is true that all beings are intrinsically connected energetically, we each have a unique path to follow that will create a unique perspective and sense of reality. Therefore, expecting anyone to fully understand another's perspective is unrealistic and leads to much suffering as we struggle to grasp how others could be so blind to the impact of their behavior. Peace of mind cannot exist within the act of struggle, and perpetuating struggle through repeatedly trying to understand the behavior of others disturbs the flow of acceptance and allowance that generates peace. And so it is important that you understand that the longer you sit within the struggle of trying to understand, or churning the memory of the incident in your mind, or imagining revenge, you will move further and further away from that state of acceptance and allowance and continue to perpetuate an energy of disquietude.

It is your natural state of being as an energetic entity to be at peace, and so when your emotions and the thoughts that occur in reaction to them disturb the flow of the peaceful state, you will find that you feel out of sorts in your physical body and in your mental and energetic being. If you remain in that state long enough, you will find that you will create a habit of thinking that evolves into one of victimization; in this belief you will begin to blame other people, your life circumstances, and your environment for your state of unease, and you will move further away from the truth, which is that only you can direct the course that will return you to your natural condition of ease. Here is where the struggle begins and ensues. It may be triggered by external events, but it lives within your response to them, and only you have control over those responses.

It is in the moment of taking responsibility for your own happiness that your true power lies. If you are finding that you are in a habit of negative responses to external triggers, you must first become aware of those responses and observe them, noticing what is happening in your physical body, in your mind, in your words and your tone. This is not always easy when you are in an emotional state, but it is always possible in hindsight. Next, understand that this response was a choice. It only appeared automatic because you have created a habit of response and you have not acted to intercede and deflect this habit. Ask yourself what you could have chosen that would have been better aligned with your intention for peace of mind. Was there a way for you to state your case without perpetuating the conflict? Would it have been better to simply say nothing? Could your response have been delayed until your emotions were allowed to settle? Was it really necessary for you to struggle to prove that you are right?

This type of self-examination can go a long way toward breaking old habits of reaction and creating more thoughtful and careful acts of response. And understanding that while we may be hurt, disappointed, or frustrated by the behavior of others, it is only because we have set up expectations for their behavior that are based on our own personal experience and views of the world. Once we understand that it is our expectations that are not being met, we can perhaps choose to alter those expectations to include the notion that we are not able to see through the eyes and experiences of others, and therefore we cannot project our personal perspective on them.

Shifting this sense of responsibility for your feelings away from the behavior of others and back to your own response to those behaviors will go a long way toward allowing you to forgive, release, and learn from perceived hurts. And allowing yourself to examine what there is to learn from these experiences can help you find the gift that is inherent in every encounter, as all interactions with others provide the opportunity for us to see ourselves more clearly in the mirror of another's eyes.

5. HOW DO I MAKE PEACE WITH MYSELF WHEN I KNOW I HAVE HURT, INJURED, OR DAMaGED ANOTHER? HOW DO I HEAL THE HURTS THAT I INflICT UPON MYSELF?

Understand that there is nothing you can do that will damage your soul essence. This core aspect of your being will continue to shine in all its brilliance and perfection as an extension of Source energy no matter what actions you choose in your physical life.

That being said, it is once again essential to acknowledge that your current life experience will be dependent upon your choices. If you find yourself in a state of suffering, it is in those moments that you can become acutely aware of this truth. The choices that will determine your state of being, your trajectory to your future, and the energy you emit may be choices of thought, action, words, and expression. When you find that you have made an error in one of these choices, once again it will be in your choice of response to that error that will either move you back toward your innate peace of mind or away from it.

We would like you to consider, for a moment, that a loved one has come to you in a state of distress with the dilemma of having created a conflict with another, either through an error of judgment, an emotional reaction, or a sense of revenge. How would you advise this loved one? Would you chastise and berate her, criticize her, be angry with her? Or would you be gentle, kind, and conciliatory, telling her that it is human nature to make mistakes in judgment and that forgiving herself is surely in order? Here, then, is proof that you carry the answers to your own dilemmas within; it is simply in the skewed belief system that you find the need to chastise or punish yourself for things you feel you have done wrong.

Taking an expanded perception of the situation is the required first step in seeing it clearly. This may not be possible while in the throes of conflict, but once you are able to come to a state of calm awareness, we would suggest that you find an inner perspective of detachment, just as if the scenario were played out in the life of someone else. See if you can view the conflict through the eyes of another, and gauge your reaction based on the perspective of the observer, rather than as a personal experience. This wider vantage point can lend an enormous amount of clarity, as you will find that your vision is no longer affected by the confusion of emotion and jumbled thinking.

Within that clarity may come the truth behind your behavior; you may see that you were not necessarily acting in response to the actions of another, but were acting in an egoic state of self-protection and self-righteousness. If you can understand that this is a learned response, and that the ego has been programmed to protect the psyche from a perceived threat, whether it is a realistic threat or not, you may begin to understand that you have the power to override this learned behavior and come to a better sense of truth within yourself.

The ego is an important aspect of self-awareness; it is what allows us to experience and respond to the physical incarnation with free will and deliberate intention. But it is not always an accurate barometer of truth, as it will tend to perceive threats to its existence that are something else entirely, and it will often react to those threats with emotion or defensive acts of self-preservation. If one is not at peace with oneself, one will be more prone to these delusions of threat. We have found that the lack of self-love and self-respect is directly proportional to the level of belief that perpetuates fear and defensive behavior. Those who are genuinely at peace with themselves will rarely perceive the behavior of others as a threat, and will have less of a defensive reaction to a perceived slight.

And so if you can understand that your act of hurting another stemmed from a sense of deficiency within yourself, perhaps you can begin to take steps toward correcting that belief system to one that is more empowering, that is sturdy enough in its strength of awareness that it does not need to perpetuate fearful or defensive behavior, and that will thereby change future responses to those that are rooted in compassion.

Of course, the next crucial step will be forgiveness, and it is only within the understanding that forgiveness is the same as release that you will begin to learn how to forgive yourself and others. It is not an act of excusing hurtful behavior; it is, however, an act of love and compassion that understands that the incarnate experience is one of learning through one's errors in judgment, that the physical life requires that mistakes be made in order that we may learn to correct them, and that the universe does not judge these mistakes, nor will we be punished for them, as it is understood that the road we have chosen for this physical experience will, by design, have multiple opportunities for us to choose our responses, and we are bound to make some choices that are not in the best interests of ourselves and others.

It is also important to understand that all the players on the stage of your life have also made choices that have led them to the circumstances surrounding the event that has caused conflict, and that they will also have the opportunity to choose their response to the situation. As such, there can be outcomes of the situation that will greatly benefit them, should they choose to perceive the gift behind the hurt.

It is through the process of perspective, awareness, forgiveness, allowance, and acceptance that you may choose to return to your natural peaceful state of being.

6. HOW DOES ONE MAKE PEACE WITH THEIR PHYSICAL BODY WHEN IT SEEMS TO CAUSE THEM SO MUCH PAIN, STRUGGLE, OR EVEN DISGUST? WHAT DO THEY NEED TO DO TO FEEL THE TRUE BLESSING OF THEIR PHYSICAL NATURE AND STOP STRUGGLING WITH IT?

The first step is to understand that you do not struggle against your own intrinsic ideas of what your physical form should look like or act like, but against a learned ideal that is culturally conditioned and based on the whims of a few who decide that they can dictate the way a society perceives beauty and worthiness. This self-critical nature stems from a belief system that says we have to conform to these cultural standards, and if we don't, we will be cast out. In actuality, it is you who do the casting out.

Because physical beings rely so much on their five senses to experience reality, there is a lot of emphasis on the way things look. These visual cues are what keep you safe; they will keep you away from things that repulse you and draw you to things that are intrinsically attractive. There are built-in instincts within the brains of all creatures to respond to that which is perceived with the five senses, and it is by design that you are naturally attracted to some things and compelled to avoid others.

There are, however, some aspects of this process that are learned, such as the idea of beauty. When you examine other cultures and time periods, you will find that the standards of beauty shift and change, especially when it comes to what is considered desirable in the human form. We would suggest that you consider this and ask where this standard originates. Is it an instinctual function of the brain, or is it another learned belief based on what is culturally accepted as truth? Can you override these learned beliefs and create your own that are more resonant with what you believe to be true about beauty and the nature of the human form?

Herein lies the struggle between what you know to be true in your heart and what is conditioned as truth in your thinking. Your five senses tend toward the latter; they are directly connected to the intellectual process of logic and reason, and it is in those brain functions that you will find the learned belief system that has become an automatically programmed truth. But just as you can alter the programming of a computer, you can alter the programming of the brain to accept a different truth, one that is more resonant with your soul's wisdom and the calling of your heart.

Self-love is not something that is learned in your human culture. In fact, it is usually taught as something to be avoided; it is considered sinful and vain, and children are admonished at an early age to avoid being self-centered and self-important. And so the brain is programmed from an early age to focus on that which is flawed and needing improvement, and that which is ugly and needing to be hidden or corrected. Thus, it becomes a habit to see only that which is wrong with the body when one looks at oneself.

It is important to understand the psychology behind this self-criticism. The learned belief that has programmed the brain not only creates a way of thinking, it creates a way of SEEING the visual representation of the self. This means that what you are perceiving as yourself is a false image, viewed through the filter of a false belief system and projected onto your visual cortex as reality. You have been convinced that your eyes don't lie, but in truth, it is the interpretation of that light reflection back to the brain that is flawed, as it is being skewed by a belief system that is set to interpret any image of the self as defective.

Here are some exercises you can practice that can assist in the reprogramming of the belief system, thereby creating a different sense and truth about beauty and how you perceive the image of yourself.

Begin to become more aware of how you view the beauty of the ones you love. When you look at a child, or a dear friend, or a family member, what is it that you are seeing? Do you find yourself automatically finding those aspects of their human form that are beautiful, or are you seeking flaws? Can you acknowledge that which your society deems as defective and find the beauty in it? Do you see how your eyes will be drawn to the beauty of a loved one's face and physical form, and even find beauty in those things that your society may not dictate as beautiful?

With that knowledge in mind, look at yourself in the mirror and observe the difference in the way you view yourself. Are you seeking beauty or flaws? Do your eyes naturally look for that which needs improvement or that which is desirable? Can you find the beauty in your own perceived flaws?

And now, while the results of this exercise are fresh in your mind, create a journal entry that consists of four lists. The first list will be what you find beautiful about the physical aspect of a loved one. The second list will be what you find to be flawed about that person. The third and fourth lists will be what you find beautiful and flawed about yourself. Observe these lists, meditate on them, and set the intention that they become more balanced in their perspective.

Focusing on the lists about you, see if you can move one thing each day from the list of flaws onto the list of beauty. Do not just do this as a rote exercise; really focus on each thing that you find as flawed and feel its intrinsic beauty. Each time you move one item over, bless it, make peace with it, love the beauty within the flaw, and set the intention to release the programmed judgment that creates so much struggle within you.

Also set the intention, through this exercise, to understand the value of perspective. When one is in the midst of a life crisis or tragedy, one can only respond with emotion and cannot see the lesson or gift within the circumstance. It is only through time that perspective can be gained and the gift revealed. The same holds true with the image of the self. When one is experiencing life in the first person, one is often blind to the external perspective, which can be much softer, kinder, and wiser. Here is where detachment is key; allowing yourself to detach from that which you have learned to be truth, creating a new truth that is more in line with the truth you hold for others, and practicing a perspective that steps outside the programmed intellect and into the higher truth will reset the reactive visual interpretation of the self into a more truthful image of that which is beautiful, divine, and representative of the universal soul being.

7. WHAT IS THE BEST WAY TO fiND BALaNCE IN MY LIFE? THeRe NEVeR SEeMS TO BE ENOUGH TIME TO DO ALl THE THINGS I WANT TO DO. HOW CAN I CREATE THE TIME?

Here again, you must become clear about what you want. It is all well and good to desire a more balanced life, but if you are asking for balance and yet fearful of letting go of anything in your life, your attempts at creating time for the things you'd like to manifest will not be very successful.

Understand that physical beings often hold on to physical things out of fear. They will also hold on to responsibilities, relationships, obligations, and habits because these things have become part of their identity and they fear who they will become without even one of those things. However, holding on to a lot of extraneous things that do not resonate with you can only create an anchor to the past that will keep you from moving forward into your future and enjoying what is right now.

If you are feeling that your life and time are unbalanced, it is essential that you look at where you are spending your time and energy with the intention of lightening the load. This may cause some fear, as you will resist letting go of anything that appears to be a means to an end; however, it is essential that you find ways to cut back the amount of time you are spending on those things that can be delegated to others or eliminated altogether.

Often the imbalance is created by a lack of self-care and a failure to include recreation and rest in your schedule with the same amount of priority as work. When work and income become the primary goals in deciding how you spend your days, you will find that eventually you will begin to feel resentful of this neglect, resulting in fatigue, irritability, and discontent. It is essential to the health of the mind, body, and spirit that you tend to their needs with just as much care as you tend to others and your work.

The importance of lighthearted and creative activities cannot be emphasized enough. Without them, you may begin to feel a sense of malaise and disappointment. The spirit within you cries out for peaceful interludes that nurture and care for it, and for creative expression, even if that expression never amounts to anything more than a hobby.

And so, if you find that you are spending an inordinate amount of time on obligations, work, and caring for others, and a disproportionately small amount of time on yourself, you may want to ask yourself these questions:

1. How can I better manage my day so that I get more accomplished in a shorter amount of time? Is it possible to consolidate some of my obligations, or delegate them to someone else?

2. Can I schedule at least one day per week that is devoted solely to myself and my family? Can I make sure to stick to the policy of no work on this day, unless it is an emergency?

3. Can I find at least a few minutes at the end of the day to journal about my feelings, my desires, and my intentions? (This can be very helpful in drawing your highest good toward you. It will also distract you from some of the worries and concerns that may be the outcome of an overworked individual.)

4. Is there a way to integrate some self-care into my daily schedule? Can I spend two minutes of a bathroom break in meditation? Can I take a walk at lunchtime? Can I call or text to connect with a loved one sometime during the day, simply because I know it will pick me up? Can I be sure to take frequent stretch and bend breaks from sitting at my keyboard for hours on end?

You also need to be sure that you are balancing your home life with your social life and your intellect with your heart. The first step is to make peace with where you are. Be grateful for your busy life, as it means you are attracting many opportunities for fulfillment and appreciation and that you have achieved a sense of being needed and appreciated. The second step is to learn to say NO to those opportunities that weigh heavily on you and become burdensome. If you have already scheduled time for yourself and another invitation arrives, be sure that you are seeing that scheduled time as a priority, and that you do not fall into the trap of constantly putting the needs of others before your own.

Learning to say NO to opportunities that will overburden you or that simply do not resonate with you, setting clear time constraints on projects and activities so that you are getting a lot done within a short amount of time, delegating things that do not have to be in your control, asking for help when it is needed, making self-care a priority, and finding time throughout your day for continual self-care are all ways to achieve a more balanced, productive, and fulfilled life.

8. WHERE DO OUR LOVED ONES IN SPIRIT GO AND WHY DO THEY HAVE TO LEAVE US? HOW CAN WE MAKE PEACE WITH OUR GRIEF AND THE PAIN OF MISSING THEIR PRESENCE IN OUR LIVES?

We would like to make this very clear: the act of death is not a leaving, it is a transformation. Your loved ones have not abandoned you, no matter what it feels like to you without their physical presence. They have shed the physical form because it was time for them to do so, whether you choose to accept that truth or not. There is no one right way, time, or method to die; all of them are right, and all death occurs at the exact right time for the individual and with the full consent of the soul.

The challenge here has to do with the pain of the physical loss of a loved one. It is in the longing for their presence in your life that you struggle, and within that struggle may come a railing against the unfairness of it, an anger toward a God who would dare to take this person's life away from them, and a fearful reminder of one's own mortality.

It is because you hold life as so precious that you feel that the ending of it is a tragedy, and that what you would consider an untimely death is a travesty, a theft of something precious, the ultimate deception of God against human. And it is true that your physical life is a precious gift, an opportunity to revel in all the joys, pains, and sorrows that will enhance and enrich your soul, to bask in the beauty of your planet, to experience the physical delights of the senses, and to love and be loved. But your vision here is quite limited, as you fail to take into account that you are at your core a spirit being who has decided to inhabit the physical in a temporary way before returning to your natural state.

Understand that all that you experience here is temporary by design. Having the opportunity for constant change ensures that you have the best chance of evolving, learning, and growing into the realization of your own creative power, and that you can experience healing of grief, pain, and loss as you move forward in time and create a new way of living. It is not an easy thing to make peace with the passing of a loved one, as you will feel their absence as pain, but if you can come to terms with the truth—that these loved ones have returned to their natural state in a sacred and divine dimensional space that is full of beauty, love, and grace, and from which they can still see you, commune with your energy, and support your journey—you may find that your grief is softened and that your sadness is less all-encompassing with time.

We would suggest that you set the intention to create a different relationship with the concept of death, and understand that the way you have been taught to view it is not necessarily the truth. As you come to understand that all things in this physical existence are transient, that they will ebb and flow with the tides, and that nothing in the physical can be fully grasped and anchored in place, you will more easily make peace with the nature of all things, people, and experiences in your life as they flow through you. Every experience, every person, and every challenge presents the opportunity for divine expression and connection, especially in the death of a loved one, who passes into the true divine essence of their soul as they transition back to their original state and shed the heaviness of the physical being.

Understand that just as the energy of the soul and spirit is eternal, so is the energy of love, and that no perceived slights, hurts, or conflicts will be carried over into the spirit realm, as these things have no place there. As the physical shell is shed, so are all maladies, pains, and restrictions of the body, as well as any suffering, confusion, or trauma. Your loved ones do not sit in judgment of you, nor do they feel anger or disappointment with anything that happened while they were in the physical experience. They only feel love, even if they never expressed that love in their lifetime. Love is all that's left when the negativity of a wounded ego is shed.

We would suggest that when you are experiencing the grief of loss, that you take some time to imagine your loved ones transitioning into their natural state of energetic spirit. Can you visualize them free and unencumbered, with great joy in their reunion with their own loved ones in spirit, and free of any physical, emotional, or mental pain that was experienced in their lifetime? Can you feel the joy in this transition and know that they are not only at peace, but in a state of euphoria like nothing you could experience on Earth? Can you imagine the beauty of this transition as it is filled with loving energy, divine beings, and a joyful welcome home? Here, then, is the truth of death: It is a joyous occasion for all and one that is filled with light, and if you can bring just a bit of that light into your heart as you grieve, you will most assuredly find comfort.

Your loved ones do not need you to honor them with your grief. They want to see you happy and moving forward with the adventure of your life. Holding on to your sadness is not a way to remember them; they wish you to remember the joyful times you had with them on this plane of existence and understand that their joy in their transitioned state far transcends any joy they could have experienced here on the physical plane. There is no need for you to wear your grief as a cloak that prevents you from enjoying the richness of your own life. This is not to say that you will not miss the physical presence of your loved one and feel periods of sadness, but understand that you can transcend this sadness and focus on the joy of gratitude that they chose to share their life with you for whatever amount of time that was allowed, and create a legacy of the love and happiness that you shared while they were here.

Grief will come, sadness will come, loss will come—they are inevitable aspects of the physical experience. The choice that you are being offered is about what you will do with those emotions, how you will allow them to shape your life and soul, what you will find out about yourself through these feelings, and how, through your connection to divine will and Source energy, you will carry on, thrive, and return to happiness.

9. How do I get back in touch with the child in me who used to experience life as a joyful adventure, full of wonder and love? How do I, as an adult, become childlike again?

Just as your soul is the embodiment of all aspects of your being, all lifetimes, all dimensional spaces, all personalities, and experiences, your spirit, which animates the physical in this life-time, is the embodiment of all ages, all experiences, and all stages of evolution within the lifetime. As such, the child is very much alive and well within you; it has simply been pushed aside by the need to fulfill obligations, become a responsible adult, and reflect a persona that is mature and serious.

We would very much like to advocate that you commune with this childlike aspect of your being on a daily basis.

We are drawn to the energy of children because of the pure and bright energy that surrounds them. They are motivated by curiosity and wonder, and the desire to feel joy and connection. They spend very little time absorbed in the past or worried about the future, and can become so acutely focused on the present moment in the act of creative play that all else around them fades into the background. It is in those moments that their physical, mental, and spiritual aspects are fully engaged in a harmonic act of self-expression, and they are building upon that creative act as part of the creation of life itself. It is here that source energy speaks through us, in the creative aspect of being, whether that creative act produces a crayon drawing or a great work of art, a toy assemblage or a suspension bridge, an imagined meal or a feast for thousands. The energy that surrounds the creative act is the divine expression of Source at its finest, and even when we are simply witnesses to this energy, we are moved.

Here, then, is the key: The act of playful creation comes naturally to children, and to the childlike aspect that continues to live within your being. We would encourage you to explore this aspect of yourself on a regular basis. What creative spark lives within you? Was there once something you loved to do but gave it up in favor of more practical pursuits? Did you once love to draw, or sculpt, or play music? Did you spend hours creating dialogues between your toys, or imagining great adventures in the park? Did you transform the elements around you into a beautiful land of mystical marvels and mythical creatures? And do you ever find yourself being pulled into similar daydreams now, only to push them aside as frivolous or a waste of time?

No act of creativity is ever wasted, make no mistake about that. It is within those moments of creativity that we are able to engage with the divine and create a flow of energy that allows us to experience ourselves as masters of our life's experience and extensions of the supreme creative energy of Source. Playing expands your energetic field and creates a feeling of euphoric joy, and within that emotional and energetic state lies the key to the transformation of your life toward the highest aspects of your being. It ignites the processes of the brain and integrates those processes with the calling of the heart, which is the expression of the spirit. It is what arranges the energetic qualities of matter into reality, and aligns the circumstances of life into action. Never underestimate the power of this force, as it is what helped to create you as you are today.

And so we would recommend that you bring more playtime into your life. Any act of creativity can be considered play, whether it is artistic, literary, verbal, culinary, constructive, physical, or mental. Passive entertainment such as listening to music or watching TV are restful, but creating your own music or stories is active, and it is within this action that you truly engage the creative aspect of yourself. Do it more. Make something, no matter how well you think you can do it. Make something without judgment, just for the sheer joy of it. Make something until you develop a passion for making it that will then translate into the passion for creating your life, creating joy, creating love. Make something until you realize that this is who you are and why you came here—to create, to choose, to form your life with your own will and your own divine spark. You are a creator, a maker, a divine extension of all the creative energy of the universe. What are you going to do with this supreme power? We would highly recommend that you find a way to have fun with it. And it is within that fun that you will once again engage the child within, in wonder and amazement for all that this life has to offer you.

10. How Do I Access TRUTH? How Do I Know What Is TRUTHFUL AND REAL WHEN THERe Is SO MUCH UNTRUTH SURROUNDING ME?

Just as the child lives within you, so does all knowing, all wisdom, and all truth, as you are at your core a direct extension of Source, of universal wisdom, of the all-knowing mind. So even though this wisdom is not always apparent to you, it is there, it is available, and it can be accessed to help guide you through the path of your life.

You may have had experiences in your life where you've witnessed the sage wisdom of a child, whose physical nature seems to portray a helplessness and dependency on the maturity of an adult to guide her. This child may have surprised you on occasion with some supreme wisdom about the nature of life, or some resonant truth that shook you to the core and made you think of yourself or your life in a different way. This child was, in that moment, connecting with that inner wisdom, to that infinite source of knowing, without the filter of learned beliefs and the self-protective ego. There can be much wisdom gained through the open channel of a child.

And so, you can see that as we mature, we accumulate a great deal of false beliefs and heavy trappings of ego that block our innate connection to divine wisdom and truth. We place great obstacles in the way of this free-flowing energetic connection, and then we wonder why it is that we are having difficulty figuring out our lives. The wisdom that you believe to be practical and intellectual—while it has its place in the world—is not usually your best guide when it comes to connecting with your soul's path and fulfilling the joyful trajectory that you planned for this life.

Understand that every time you find a reason why you cannot fulfill a dream to follow the calling of your heart, you are blocking that inner wisdom. Every time you judge yourself to be unworthy or not good enough, you are constructing more walls to your energetic connection to the truth. Every time you look to another person, achievement, or possession to create happiness in your life, you are ignoring what you know to be true about needing to first create within what you wish to experience in the external world. Whenever you find yourself mired in the intellectual and practical aspects of your life, you are ignoring that energetic aspect that is your direct line to truth and wisdom.

Therefore, it is imperative that you find a way to stretch your thinking into the realms of the unknown, that you extend your focus beyond that which you can experience with the five senses, that you feel the energetic and emotional expressions of yourself just as authentically as you feel the physical, and that you experience this energy through gratitude, through joy, and through the loving nature of your spirit being. The freedom that you can experience by breaking down the walls of conformed thinking is what will lead you to the truth of who you are and why you are here.

In other words, stop trying so hard to figure it all out. Your brain was not created for this pastime. It is the processor that allows you to make sense of the physical experience; it is not designed to grasp the nonphysical nature of being, as it is by its very nature intrinsically physical and rooted in its physically generated energy. While it is an amazing and miraculous part of your being, it is limited just by the nature of its physicality, and therefore, it will limit your experience if you rely solely on it to guide and inform you.

Beyond the thinking brain lies the energetic nature of your being. Consider this: You would not rely on the physical nature of a wire to define its purpose; it is the electricity flowing through the wire that is the intrinsic truth of the nature of the wire. Without that energy, it is simply physical matter that takes up space. But with that energy, it is a conduit for light, for motion, for creative action. Your brain and the rest of your physical body are like that wire. While they are miraculous feats of creation in and of themselves, it is the energy that runs through them that defines the nature of their purpose.

And so, restricting your comprehension of the nature of reality and the truth of being to that which you have learned, that which you can see, and that which you can experience comfortably is ignoring an entire realm of being that goes beyond what you can easily comprehend or explain in a logical way. Embrace that fact, that there will be things you cannot comprehend within the limitations of the physical brain but that you can feel as resonant truth. There are moments of inspired intuition that defy the logic of scientific thought but that bring you to a state of grace and wisdom that cannot be achieved solely through the workings of the brain. You have experienced these moments of insight and intuition at various times in your life, and you have probably found a way to explain them in a logical sense so that you are more comfortable with them. But the reality is that it is within these moments that you are truly connected with the divine energetic aspect of who you really are.

This is why meditation and other forms of mindfulness are so effective in helping you experience that energetic connection. As you focus on being in the moment, as you retrieve your thoughts from dwelling in the past or future, as you allow your frequency to rise and connect, you will discover that this clear channel was always open to you, and that once you clear away the blockages to it, you will find that it is more easily accessible to help guide and comfort you on your path.

This does not mean, however, that those who practice mindfulness will never find themselves at odds with their path and in a state of quandary or indecision, for it is within these states that you are able to exercise your divine will to make choices. If these choices are based solely on what you can see and what you can think, they may not always lead you to your intended state of being. This, in and of itself, is not an error, for it will be part of the journey toward an evolved state of being. But as you find yourself in a place on your path that is not resonant with your inner sense of truth, it is important to acknowledge how you arrived there and what sense of inner knowing you were ignoring along the way.

We all receive intuitive information on a regular basis. This is the knowing force that gives us a sense of resonance with truth. We will feel that someone is not who they appear to be, or that a situation is not as it seems. We will feel the energy of a connection as being beneficial or not, despite what the intellect is telling us. We will sense that something needs to be avoided, or that something is calling us forward that is not based on a logical process. It is through the quiet acknowledgment of these feelings and senses that we can more strongly connect with the innate truths of our soul's wisdom, and we can quiet the alarms of logical thought that are not always in our best interest and that can steer us away from our inner truths.

WHAT ARE 10 QUESTIONS THAT YOU WOULD ASK OF A MoRE ADVANCED CIVILIZATION? AND THEN COULD YOU PLEASE AN— SWER THOSE QUESTIONS AS IF WE HAD ASKED THEM OF YOU?

What we would like to point out initially is that there are many different types of advancement when it comes to individual beings, societies, and civilizations, and so when one is referring to a "more" advanced civilization, we would wonder what type of advancement it is that makes this civilization comparatively superior. Is it their technological advances? Their advances in social living, environmental care, compassionate justice, intel- lectual capacity, spiritual awareness, or, perhaps, an evolutionary advancement that includes all of these? We have encountered a fair number of civilizations at various levels of advancement in all of these areas, and we would not categorize any of them as neces- sarily superior or inferior to our society or yours. Rather, they are simply at a different place in their evolution, which will inevitably be different for every species of being.

However, we can conjecture that your definition of superior advancement includes all the areas mentioned, and so we will pro- ceed with some rumination based on that.

1. WHAT, IF ANYTHING, DO YOU FEeL YOU SACRIFiCED IN THE NAME OF SCIENTIFiC, TECHNOLOGICAL, oR INTELlECTUAL AD— VANCEMeNTS? DO YOU FEeL THERe WERe LOSSES oR A SENSE OF DISCONnECTION FROM OTHER FoRMS OF YOUR SOCIETY'S LIVES SUCH AS A CONnECTION TO THE NATURAL ENVIRONMENT, RITUAL, SPIRITUAL DEVeLOPMENT, FAMILY LIFE, oR A SENSE OF RECREATION AND AMUSEMeNT? AND IF THERe WERe SACRI— FiCES MADE IN ANY OF THESe AREAS, WAS THE ADVANCEMeNT OF YOUR SPECIES IN OTHER AREAS WoRTH THE LOSs?

There was a time when the scientific advancements of our civilization became more important and more respected than any other view on the nature of reality. As such, we lost touch with the more spiritual aspects of interconnectedness, love, compassion, and self-respect. We became so absorbed in the search for what we felt was concrete reality—based on the truth that we believed was limited by what we could experience through our own physical senses—that we began to see the consequences of our actions on the fate of the planet and all its inhabitants. It was only when we took an expanded view of science that included the spiritual nature of reality that we started to shift back to a more compassionate, mindful, and conscious species. And so we are convinced that a narrow view of reality that is based solely on what can be "proven," while sometimes necessary and fruitful, negates a huge portion of reality that goes beyond those theories and experiments and explores the nature of the soul being and conscious energy.

2. HAS YOUR SCIENTIFIC COMMUNITY INTEGRATED THE STUDY OF THE SPIRITUAL REALMS INTO ITS FIELDS OF RESEARCH AND, IF SO, HOW HAS THIS CHANGED YOUR SOCIETY? IF THERE WAS RESISTANCE TO THIS STUDY, HOW DID YOU OVERCOME IT? AND HOW HAS THIS FIELD OF STUDY AFFECTED THE BELIEF SYSTEMS OF YOUR GENERAL POPULATION?

See the above for part of this answer. There was quite a bit of resistance to this new sense of reality, especially among those whose lives were dedicated to scientific research and theory. There were many egos that needed shifting during this phase, as their identities were threatened by the perceived negation of their work. It was only when it was understood that this was truly an expansion of their work, not a dismissal of it, that minds began to open and different types of theories began to emerge. As you are experiencing on your planet at this time, there will always be those who feel threatened by change, and who will do anything within their power to negate it, especially when it feels threatening to their perception of reality. Gentle, compassionate persistence is needed during these times, as force will only cause more vigilant resistance. There remains among us a small group of what you may refer to as anarchists who steadfastly cling to some of the old beliefs, despite many of the advances that have been experienced through the new field of study. These groups live largely separate and isolated from the general population, and their numbers are dwindling as the centuries go by.

3. HOW DO YOU VALUE THE WORK OF OTHERS? IN A HIGHLY EVOLVED SOCIETY, ARE THERE STILL THOSE WHO CONTRIBUTE IN WHAT MAY BE CONSIDERED MENIAL OR PHYSICAL-LABOR JOBS, OR ARE THERE AUTOMATED SYSTEMS THAT HAVE TAKEN THE PLACE OF MANPOWER? HOW DO YOUR CITIZENS OCCUPY THEMSELVES AND fiND VALUE AND PURPOSE IN THEIR LIVES?

Our structure is based largely on a system of exchange, which allows the time, energy, and expertise of each individual to be rewarded by an equal amount of energy, through trades of services and goods.

In a practical sense of energetic measurement, and in the experience of energy from an incarnated standpoint, an "equal amount of energy" would be measured in time and space. As a form of energetic exchange, one would consider the amount of time, skill, and physical materials that went into the work being performed. For instance, if a repair is made to a structure, consideration would be given to the time put into that repair, the materials used, and the skill level of the individual performing the job. If this individual is an expert at this type of work, the value of the work would be in accordance with that skill set; if the individual were an apprentice or beginner, the expectation of the quality of that work may be lower and, as such, so would the value. And so, consideration would be placed upon what would be a fair energetic exchange in terms of time, skill, and quality of work. This craftsman could expect an exchange in the form of some good or service that required a similar amount of time, expertise, and quality as that which he expended.

Of course, value is a very subjective term. When one is in need of something, its value to that individual increases, and so it may sometimes occur that this scale of time, skill, and quality is not exactly equal in the exchange, but as it is determined and agreed upon by the parties who are participating in the exchange, there is no sense of it being dissimilar. As such, an example may be that the craftsman who performs a repair that requires a full day of work and a fair amount of materials may find equality in the exchange of a food-preparation service that may not take as much time and may entail fewer materials but has equal value, as it is something he is unable to provide for himself and it is something that he prizes. So the "equal amount of energy" is not always a logical exchange, but rather it is subject to the sense of value one places on the service or goods.

In this way, it is similar to the monetary system, which often values certain things in a way that is separate from the time, skill, and quality of the item, and focuses on the desirability of that which is being offered. But with the absence of the intervention of money, the value is determined in agreement between the two parties, and not by some external entity.

As this system has evolved, the sense of a rigid exchange of equal time, energy, and talent has loosened, and we have found that the elimination of monetary exchange has allowed those who were only poorly compensated to be more valued, and their skills better rewarded without the judgment that the symbolic structure of money could place on it. Therefore, there is a much greater sense of equality among those whose energy contributes to the well-being of society, and less of a sense of privilege and poverty. Those who are unable to contribute in a physical way find other ways to be of service, and those who are unable to participate at all are cared for without being trivialized or pitied. These types of transactions have created benefits that we could not foresee, and it has truly incited one of the most amazing shifts that we have experienced on our planet.

4. WHAT ARE YOU STILL STRIVING FOR? WHAT DILEmMAS OCCUPY THE GREAT MINDS OF YOUR SOCIETY? HAVE YOUR PEOPLE GOTTEN BETTER AT SELF-CARE AND SELF-LOVE, AND HOW DO YOU EXPRESS YOUR INDIVIDUALITY WITHIN THE SOCIAL STRUCTURE?

There is another question within the pages of this book that deals with some of the current dilemmas we face, but what we would like to stress here is that there will always be dilemmas, issues, and conflicts in a physical society and among its people. This is not because we are failing to address them or because we are not acting correctly in our striving for betterment and higher consciousness, but it is in the very nature of the incarnated life that we face these issues, as it is within the striving for solutions that we find our purpose and in the mistakes and missteps that we experience the gift of learning and enlightenment. There is no sense in striving for perfection, but there is always something to be gained in looking for solutions that create more of a sense of humanity, compassion, equal treatment, and acknowledgment of each individual, while emphasizing the connection of all beings as one. As such, we no longer look at problems or dilemmas as evidence of failure, but simply as new areas in which to grow and learn.

5. WHAT ROLE DO LOVE AND PARTNERSHIP PLAY IN YOUR SOCIETY? DO YOU STILL fiND THAT A FAMILY STRUCTURE IS THE BEST WAY FOR INDIVIDUALS TO fiND A SENSE OF STABILITY AND SUPPORT, OR IS THERE ANOTHER TYPE OF STRUCTURE THAT WORKS BETTER?

As already discussed, we maintain a family structure in our society, but it is a bit broader than the one that seems to be most prevalent in your own world, although we are seeing evidence of your own expansion of the definition of family to include previously unheard-of types of structures. Here, we allow for structures outside of the idea of a two-parent or monogamous relationship, and often there are family structures that do not necessarily limit their members to what you would term blood relations. There are different types of group living arrangements that work well for some individuals, while others prefer a more solitary or smaller family unit. All are accepted as legitimate and respected ways of life, and our young are often cared for by the larger community, as well as by the singular parents. Because our reproductive system differs from your own, we do not have as much emphasis on coupled living, although it can be chosen by those who prefer it. What is most important is that the individual's choice is supported and honored, and that any who find themselves alone and in need of assistance will receive it.

6. WHAT ASPIRATIONS DO YOU HAVE FOR YOUR FUTURE GENERATIONS? WHERE DO YOU HOPE YOUR CHILDREN WILL FIND PASSION, PURPOSE, AND FOCUS IN THEIR LIVES? AND WHAT ARE THE HINDRANCES TO THAT?

We are quite hopeful that future generations will be focused on self-expression and the fulfillment of their innermost passions and desires. We have certainly come a long way toward this type of lifestyle, especially since the advent of a nonmonetary society; however, there will sometimes exist a judgment of what work is considered useful and practical and what is sometimes seen as frivolous and unnecessary. As such, the more creative beings sometimes face a stigma of not being authentically contributing to the good of society if they are not directly providing a good or service that is necessary to the health, well-being, and advancement of others. Many among us are able to see the power of the creative force as just as necessary and vital to the well-being of our society, but there are those whose practical mindset is quite detrimental to the self-confidence of those who are more creatively influenced in their chosen field. And so, we will continue to strive toward a more open and encouraging society toward the arts of all types, and will continue to encourage those who find their gifts in these areas that need to be expressed in some way among those who wish to experience them.

7. HOW DO YOU RESOLVE CONFLICT BETWEEN LEADERS OR COMMUNITIES? HOW HAVE YOU OVERCOME ISSUES OF VIOLENCE AND WARFARE? DOES THIS TYPE OF AGGRESSION STILL EXIST IN YOUR WORLD?

We have come a long way in this area, but we have also come to understand that violence and aggression are part of the incarnated experience, and that there will always be those among us who are unable to control these and similar urges. As such, there are isolated incidents of violence in our society, usually perpetrated by those who are experiencing some type of psychological distress, or who have been wronged themselves in some way. As we continue to advance in the fields of psychological study, and we continue to develop methods for helping those with an aggressive nature to express their needs in a nonviolent way, we find that these incidents are less common. Our societal structure has never been one that was nationalized; this has not been something that we have ever found useful to our social structure, and while there are different forms of communities and different areas of the planet that are inhabited, separated by large expanses of uninhabited land, there has never been a need to fight over these parcels of land, nor have we ever seen these different communities as anything other than separate groups of the same types of individuals. As a result, we have not had the issues of land ownership, racism, or religious extremism that you have experienced on your planet. This does not mean that we have always lived in a sense of peace and harmony, however, as during the times of our greatest challenges, there existed those who acted out of a sense of desperation, much like those who experience poverty and hunger can react in your own world. Since those systems have changed, much of this sense of poverty and hunger has been eliminated; as such, the prevalence of violent crime has also diminished. Again, this is an area in which we have progressed enormously, but is also one that continues to need attention and compassionate action.

8. HAVE YOU PHYSICALLY TRAVELED TO OTHER PLANETS, SUCH AS EARTH? HAVE YOU BEEN RESEARCHING OTHER LIFE-FORMS? AND IF SO, WHAT HAVE SOME OF YOUR FINDINGS TOLD YOU?

Although we believe that our species once migrated to this planet many millennia ago from one that was dying, we have not physically traveled to other worlds. Our scientific study has been directed toward solving and alleviating the issues on our own planet and among our own people; as such, it has always been decided that our time and energy would not be best spent on space exploration. Once we were able to harness the power of the spirit to extend itself through the vast expanses of space, we did not feel it necessary to spend a lot of time and energy on physical space travel, and so it has not been something we have focused on, although it is something that interests us and we are quite curious about others who have done so.

9. HOW DO YOU HAVE FUN? WHAT PASTIMES ARE PREVALENT IN YOUR WORLD? HAVE YOU DEVISED A SYSTEM THAT ALLOWS FOR MORE SELF-EXPLORATION, SELF-IMPROVEMENT, AND LEISURE TIME? IF SO, WHAT ARE THE MOST POPULAR WAYS FOR YOUR CITIZENS TO UTILIZE THIS TIME?

As we have settled into a system that allows for more leisure time and less focus on the need to amass wealth, we have found more leisure activities that are life-enhancing, relaxing, and enriching. Our artistic fields have grown to include many differ-ent types of material art and creation, including decorative arts, the use of color and light as artistic expression, and the more typical creative arts, which are similar to those on your planet.

We have also found a type of self-expression through body art, which can be best explained as a sort of body decoration similar to your tattoos but less permanent, and a wide array of theatrical performances, including dramatic stage arts, musical arts of all types, and different types of mental feats that entail a sort of focused intensity and energetic manipulation. While a great many people partake in these activities, there still remains among a small segment of the population a stigma surrounding those who practice them, as discussed previously. However, we find that when individuals are expressing themselves in a creative way, they often open themselves up to other types of interpersonal connection with others that can influence the way they serve society as a whole.

10. HAVE YOU ERADICATED ALL DISEASE? IF NOT, WHAT DO YOU FIND THE BIGGEST CHALLENGES TO THIS AIM? WHAT WERE SOME OF YOUR MAJOR BREAKTHROUGHS IN THIS AREA?

Again, this is an area where we have made great strides, especially in recent times since the eradication of our monetary system, but we have not completely eliminated all disease and we find that sometimes new types or mutations of disease will arise that were previously unknown. We believe that as the energetic forces of the universe are in a state of constant change and flux, this will create many different types of life-forms, including those that can cause disease within the bodies of physical beings, and so while we continue to make great strides in the areas of health, immunity, and healing, we have found the need for continual research and development in this area. Currently we are researching a type of parasite that seems to have evolved from a noninvasive and benign type of creature to one that is causing cognitive and behavioral disease among children. We are, at present, very close to a preventative measure and the eradication of this deadly species, and it is where a good deal of our research and focus have been for quite a long time.

Do you have 10 questions for us?

1. Do you realize how far you've come in the realm of evolutionary consciousness in just the past 200 or 300 years?

This is something that is quite remarkable to us; when we observe your culture from the standpoint of an observer, we see massive changes in the way compassion has grown to value the lives of all beings. The treatment of children, the elderly, aspects of labor and race, advances in health care, the eradication of poverty in many sectors, efforts to support your environment and include more spiritual upliftment in education, support of alternate lifestyles and self-expression, advances in awareness about the purity of food and diet, and a general growth of open-minded curiosity about the universe and your place in it have all grown exponentially. It is true that all of these areas still have a need to further their advancement, but we would like to point out that there have been significant changes in all these aspects of life in a relatively short period of time. We would like to ask, is this not evidence of your ability to create change and direct the course of your future?

2. Do you understand that everything you seek in the external world already exists within you?

And do you understand the immense implications of that? For herein lies the crux of your current dilemmas, whatever they may be. As you look to others for the answers, you ignore your own sense of inner knowing, your own connection to divine knowledge and Source energy, and your own ability to direct the course of your future by directing the flow of your energy. This is not something that is to be taken lightly; however, it can be approached with the utmost joy and delight, as it is what you have been looking for all your lives as individuals and as a cultural whole. The answers you seek are within; unlock your energetic potential and you will find the great joy of living.

3. ARE YOU WILLING TO RELEASE THE BELIEF THAT YOU ARE A LIMITED PHYSICAL BEING WHO MUST STRIVE FOR CERTAIN PRESCRIBED ATTAINMENTS IN A PREDETERMINED COURSE OF EXISTENCE IN ORDER TO ACHIEVE ANY LEVEL OF SUCCESS OR REWARD?

Are you ready to let go of the ideas that have been taught to you in favor of those that resonate with your inner being, and more closely link this incarnate experience with your higher spiritual aspect of being? There are many who are not feeling ready to release themselves from the anchor of awareness that is rooted in the physical, in the commonplace, in the predictability of the course that has been laid out by their ancestors and that they have determined as truth. What we are proposing in all our work with you is that you determine a new truth, that you observe the trajectory of your planet's past as evidence of how new truths have created better systems, that you continue to advance your awareness of the preciousness of life, and that you have an even greater sense of your participation in the grand design of the universe.

4. HAVE YOU HEARD THE BIRDS SINGING TODAY?

Or felt the caress of air upon your face, or the warmth of a hand in yours, or the cool grass beneath your feet? Can you bring your awareness into these simple pleasures as part of your daily habits? These small acts of appreciation will go a long way in creating the shift in your consciousness that is needed to participate in the global shift toward more awareness, more compassion, and more connection with the energy of all things.

5. WHY ARE YOU SO RESISTANT TO CHANGE?

What is it about the illusion of security and continuity that makes you feel anchored to your present reality? We would suggest that you observe all aspects of the natural world as they are in a constant state of flux, and as you are an integral part of this natural environment, your energetic state is also one of perpetual change. It is an inevitable part of your existence, and we would highly recommend that you find the same acceptance and delight in this process for your own lives as you see in your natural world.

6. WHAT WILl IT TAKE FOR YOU TO LOVE YOURSELF?

Is perfection your ideal? If so, you will forever be chasing an illusion that has been created solely in the ego, which is the seat of your individuality and thus wants you to continually strive to assert that individuality. This sense of yourself is important to the way you function in the world; however, the illusion of separation that it creates can perpetuate other illusions and ideals that are unattainable and that lead to a constant state of lack and disappointment with oneself. Loving oneself creates a healthy ego—creating a sense of balance between all the aspects of being, including the mind, spirit, ego, physical body, and heart—and this can bring you into a state of balance with all of creation and with all the beings who share your space. Within that balance lies the joy of existence and the strength and determination to rise above and learn from any challenge, no matter how great. And so, we will ask again, what will it take for you to love yourself?

7. HOW DO YOU DETERMINE YOUR SENSE OF TRUTH?

Is it what most agrees with the way you were taught or raised? Is it what your political party, or social class structure, or circle of friends, or the teachers in your life dictate to you? Are you adopting the belief systems of others as your own simply because you resist the responsibility of finding it for yourself? Do you go along with things that do not really resonate with your inner knowing simply because you feel you must align yourself with a certain sector and not feel alone or different or odd? This is a time of new truths being born, just as stars are born in the universe, each with its own chemical composition and brilliance, not dependent upon those that came before it. Do not let your brilliance be drowned out by traditions rooted in fear. You have, each within yourselves, the potential to be a trailblazer and a leader within these most fertile, creative times. How are you honoring this gift?

8. HOW DOES IT MAKE YOU FEEL TO PRACTICE ACTS OF COMPASSION AND KINDNESS?

What is the energetic exchange that occurs when you connect the energy of your heart with that of another? What exactly is that light that appears in the eyes of one who is the recipient of your love and caring? Can you even adequately describe it in words? Those things that are the most difficult to put into words are the things that need to be experienced on a regular basis in order to derive the most benefit from them. We feel that the more you activate this energetic aspect of your being, the more it affects all other energetic aspects of all other energetic beings, and it is this that creates the flow of energy toward the kind of world you are imagining for yourselves.

9. WHAT IS IT THAT YOU CONSIDER TO BE BEAUTIFUL AND WHERE HAVE THESE STANDARDS ORIGINATED?

Do you believe that you are born with standards of beauty that make you drawn to certain elements and repelled by others? And if this is the case, why is it that children are not found to have an intrinsic sense of cultural beauty? Will your child be repelled by you if you do not have a perfectly symmetrical face, or slim body, or smooth skin, or other culturally desirable features? Will your pet ignore you until you perform the daily rituals that are geared to make you more socially acceptable? We would like you to understand that you have integrated cultural standards into your perception of beauty and accepted them as your own personal truth. Might it be time to broaden this perspective?

10. AS A CHILD, DID YOU FIND ENJOYMENT DIGGING INTO THE SOIL?

Did you delight in the feel of the moist earth, or sand, or clay in your hands? Did you revel in the sense of discovery of what may be lying beneath that which you could see? Did you love finding the tiny beings or roots or pebbles hidden like treasures in the deep recesses of soil? Here, then, is your mission as an incarnate being: Continue to dig, continue to uncover the delights hidden within yourself, within the experience of life, within relationships and unions with others. Explore it all with the wonder, amazement, and curiosity of a child, even when those things that are uncovered are not desirable, for it is in the discovery of them that you can set them free.

FAREWELL, FRANK, UNTIL WE WRITE AGAIN. IT IS WITH THE DEEPEST GRATITUDE THAT I THANK YOU AND TRACY FOR ALL THE FABULOUS INFORMATION YOU'VE PROVIDED.

We are humbled and grateful for this connection and for the opportunity to share your energy, your passion, and your wisdom.

It is with great reverence that we present you with these words. Know that they come with the intention of providing loving guidance through the broad perspective of those who have not only survived similar challenges to those you are now facing, but who have found ways to thrive and transcend the limitations of the physical, the intellect, and the limited vantage point of the ego. You have chosen to incarnate into a most incredible era—one of great challenge but also one of incredible resilience and diversity, great love and compassion, and a great desire for change and evolution. The bravery and force of will that motivated you all to choose this incarnation was quite remarkable, and we hope that you can find it within yourselves to feel the full force of that inner light, that divine will, and that creative spark that is no less than that of Source itself.

Our greatest wish is that you experience the full richness of this incarnated experience, with all of its joys and sorrows, and celebrate it all, for it is nothing less than a grand miracle to exist within the physical wonder of the universe. The bright spark of your spirit will never fade. In fact, it will continue to grow brighter throughout all of your many incarnations and realms of existence, and within that spark lies the sparks of all others, all beings, all forms of life, including our own, with the ultimate connection to the love and power of Source, which animates us all. We wish you nothing but love in all its many forms as you traverse this grand adventure, and we thank you for allowing us to share this field of consciousness with you. Many blessings are sent along to your planet from us, your servants from afar.

ABOUT
THE AUTHORS

Mike Dooley is a former PricewaterhouseCoopers international tax consultant turned entrepreneur. He's the founder of a philosophical Adventurer's Club on the Internet that's now home to more than 750,000 members from 182 countries. His inspirational books emphasizing spiritual accountability have been published in 25 languages, and he was one of the featured teachers in the international phenomenon The Secret. Today Mike is best known for his free Notes from the Universe e-mailings, social network postings, and his *New York Times* bestsellers *Infinite Possibilities: The Art of Living Your Dreams* and *Leveraging the Universe: 7 Steps to Engaging Life's Magic*. Mike lives what he teaches, traveling internationally to speak on life, dreams, and happiness. For more information on Mike's work, or to receive his free daily Notes from the Universe e-mailings, please visit www.tut.com.

Tracy Farquhar, owner of the Spirit Light Center in Southern New Jersey, is a professional psychic medium, channel, psychic development teacher and coach, author of the best-selling book *Frank Talk: A Book of Channeled Wisdom*, and a Certified Infinite Possibilities Trainer and Trailblazer. She offers psychic and mediumship readings (both in person and remotely), workshops, spiritual retreats, and events. See SpiritLightServices.com for more information and join her on Facebook at facebook.com/spiritlightservices.

Hay House Titles of Related Interest

YOU CAN HEAL YOUR LIFE, the movie, starring Louise Hay & Friends
(available as a 1-DVD program, an expanded 2-DVD set,
and an online streaming video)
Learn more at www.hayhouse.com/louise-movie

THE SHIFT, the movie, starring Dr. Wayne W. Dyer
(available as a 1-DVD program, an expanded 2-DVD set,
and an online streaming video)
Learn more at www.hayhouse.com/the-shift-movie

✹✹✹

*A COURSE IN MIRACLES MADE EASY: Mastering the Journey from Fear to
Love,* by Alan Cohen

LIFE'S OPERATING MANUAL: With the Fear and Truth Dialogues,
by Tom Shadyac

UNCHARTED: The Journey through Uncertainty to Infinite Possibility,
by Colette Baron-Reid

THE UNIVERSE HAS YOUR BACK: Transform Fear to Faith,
by Gabrielle Bernstein

All of the above are available at your local bookstore,
or may be ordered by contacting Hay House (see next page).

✹✹✹

We hope you enjoyed this Hay House book. If you'd like to receive our online catalog featuring additional information on Hay House books and products, or if you'd like to find out more about the Hay Foundation, please contact:

Hay House, Inc., P.O. Box 5100, Carlsbad, CA 92018-5100
(760) 431-7695 or (800) 654-5126
(760) 431-6948 (fax) or (800) 650-5115 (fax)
www.hayhouse.com® • www.hayfoundation.org

———

Published in Australia by: Hay House Australia Pty. Ltd.,
18/36 Ralph St., Alexandria NSW 2015
Phone: 612-9669-4299 • *Fax:* 612-9669-4144
www.hayhouse.com.au

Published in the United Kingdom by: Hay House UK, Ltd.,
The Sixth Floor, Watson House, 54 Baker Street, London W1U 7BU
Phone: +44 (0)20 3927 7290 • *Fax:* +44 (0)20 3927 7291
www.hayhouse.co.uk

Published in India by: Hay House Publishers India,
Muskaan Complex, Plot No. 3, B-2, Vasant Kunj, New Delhi 110 070
Phone: 91-11-4176-1620 • *Fax:* 91-11-4176-1630
www.hayhouse.co.in

———

Access New Knowledge.
Anytime. Anywhere.

Learn and evolve at your own pace
with the world's leading experts.

www.hayhouseU.com

Notes

Notes

Printed in the United States
by Baker & Taylor Publisher Services